MW00533961

Spirits & Death in Niagara

Marcy Italiano

Schiffer Publishing Ltd®

4880 Lower Valley Road, Atglen, Pennsylvania 19310

Schiffer Books are available at special discounts for bulk purchases for sales promotions or premiums. Special editions, including personalized covers, corporate imprints, and excerpts can be created in large quantities for special needs. For more information contact the publisher:

Published by Schiffer Publishing Ltd.
4880 Lower Valley Road
Atglen, PA 19310
Phone: (610) 593-1777;
Fax: (610) 593-2002
E-mail: Info@schifferbooks.com

For the largest selection of fine reference books on this and related subjects, please visit our web site at
www.schifferbooks.com
We are always looking for people to write books on new and related subjects. If you have an idea for a book please contact us at the above address.

This book may be purchased from the publisher.
Include $3.95 for shipping.
Please try your bookstore first.
You may write for a free catalog.

In Europe, Schiffer books are distributed by
Bushwood Books
6 Marksbury Ave.
Kew Gardens
Surrey TW9 4JF England
Phone: 44 (0) 20 8392-8585;
Fax: 44 (0) 20 8392-9876
E-mail: info@bushwoodbooks.co.uk
Website: www.bushwoodbooks.co.uk
Free postage in the U.K., Europe;
air mail at cost.

Dedication

To all of those who have died in and around Niagara Falls. May the lives that they once led inspire us, teach us, and in some cases, save us from the same fate.

Also, to my husband G, for always coming on the journey. Your support means the world to me. I don't know what I'd do without you.

Acknowledgements

A HUGE thank you to...

My husband for helping me with some of the photography, always being a first reader, and climbing to places I couldn't reach;

Kyle Upton and the staff at Fort George;

Daniel and Stephanie Cumerlato from Haunted Hamilton;

My honest first readers and occasional fact checkers, Dave Hogg and Ron Dickie;

The staff at Waterloo Public Library, for not killing me when I hoarded books.

Everyone at the following websites:
   www.hauntedhamilton.com –
      Haunted Hamilton,
   http://www.torontoghosts.org –
      Toronto Ghosts and Hauntings Research Society,
   http://hauntedontario.netfirms.com –
      Haunted Ontario,
   http://theshadowlands.net/ghost/groups.htm –
      Local Ghost hunters, Investigators and Researchers,
   www.nfpl.library.on.ca –
      Niagara Falls Public Library Online,
   www.niagara-info.com –
      Tourism Information for the Niagara Region,
   www.niagarafrontier.com –
      Niagara Frontier, and
   www.infoniagara.com –
      Info Niagara

Thanks, of course, to Schiffer Books for asking me to write this book — it's been a fun ride.

Contents

Introduction

Niagara Falls definitely earns the title of one of the Wonders of the World. People from all over the earth are drawn to the beauty and power of the crashing water. It is considered to be the honeymoon capital, but the entire Niagara region is full of interesting and often extremely violent history. Dating back to when the Senecas were the only people who lived in the area, mysteries and legends about Niagara Falls were always very beautiful and extremely dangerous.

There was another writer who was drawn to Niagara Falls. Samuel Langhorne Clemens returned to America after traveling in Europe. He worked as an editor for the local newspaper and invested $25,000 in *The Buffalo Express*, with money he had earned from the sales of his book, *The Innocents Abroad*, written under his pen name, Mark Twain. In his first editorial, he wrote to the people:

"I am not going to introduce any startling reforms, or in any way make any trouble. I am simply going to do my plain, unpretending duty, when I cannot get out of it; I shall work diligently and honestly and faithfully at all times and upon all occasions, when privation and want shall compel me to do it; in writing, I shall always confide myself to the truth, except when it is attended with inconvenience; I shall witheringly rebuke all forms of crime and misconduct, except when committed by the party wearing my own vest, I shall not make use of slang of vulgarity upon any occasion or under any circumstances, and shall never use profanity except in discussing house rent and taxes. Indeed, upon second thought, I will not use it even then, for it is unChristian, inelegant, and degrading – thought to speak truly I do not see how house rent and taxes – are going to be discussed worth a cent without it. I shall not meddle in politics because we have a political editor who is already quite excellent, and only needs to serve a term in the penitentiary to be perfect. I shall not write any poetry unless I conceive a spite against the subscribers." (*Romance of Niagara*, 261)

Some people suspected that he didn't like his editorial job when he left for Elmira, New York. It was there that he met his wife, Olivia, and the two of them returned to Buffalo where her father had bought them a house as a wedding present. Sadly, tragedy also came to the Clemens' home. Within a few months Olivia's father, Mr. Langdon, died in the house. Olivia's long-time friend also died of typhoid in their home. Olivia also became quite ill after delivering their first child two months early. By 1871 the couple sold the Buffalo Express at a loss for $10,000 and moved to Cincinnati, Ohio (and five years later, he wrote Tom Sawyer).

Mark Twain was always drawn to the water. He had been a captain of a river boat on the Mississippi before the Civil War. (His pen name came from the call "Mark Twain!" used to communicate how deep the water was for their ship to pass, by marking off a weighted rope in fathoms that was lowered into the water.) During his stay in Buffalo, Twain made frequent trips to Niagara Falls and took the ferry to the Canadian side of the

Niagara River. He enjoyed walking around the ruins of the old forts and relished the tranquility while walking alongside the river.

In the dark but humorous essay he wrote in 1903 entitled "Niagara," Twain talks about going on some of the guided tours:

"When you have examined the stupendous Horseshoe Fall till you are satisfied you cannot improve on it, you return to America by the new Suspension Bridge, and follow up the bank to where they exhibit the Cave of the Winds.

"Here I followed instructions, and divested myself of all my clothing, and put on a waterproof jacket and overalls. This costume is picturesque, but not beautiful. A guide, similarly dressed, led the way down a flight of winding stairs, which wound and wound, and still kept on winding long after the thing ceased to be a novelty, and then terminated long before it had begun to be a pleasure. We were then well down under the precipice, but still considerably above the level of the river.

"We now began to creep along flimsy bridges of a single plank, our persons shielded from destruction by a crazy wooden railing, to which I clung with both hands—not because I was afraid, but because I wanted to. Presently the descent became steeper, and the bridge flimsier, and sprays from the American Fall began to rain down on us in fast increasing sheets that soon became blinding, and after that our progress was mostly in the nature of groping. Now a furious wind began in to rush out from behind the waterfall, which seemed determined to sweep us from the bridge, and scatter us on the rocks and among the torrents below. I remarked that I wanted to go home; but it was too late. We were almost under the monstrous wall of water thundering down from above, and speech was in vain in the midst of such a pitiless crash of sound.

"In another moment the guide disappeared behind the deluge, and, bewildered by the thunder, driven helplessly by the wind, and smitten by the arrowy tempest of rain, I followed. All was darkness. Such a mad storming, roaring, and bellowing of warring wind and water never crazed my ears before. I bent my head, and seemed to receive the Atlantic on my back. The world seemed going to destruction. I could not see anything, the flood poured down so savagely. I raised my head, with open mouth, and the most of the American cataract went down my throat. If I had sprung a leak now I had been lost. And at this moment I discovered that the bridge had ceased, and we must trust for a foot-hold to the slippery and precipitous rocks. I never was so scared before and survived it. But we got through at last, and emerged into the open day, where we could stand in front of the laced and frothy and seething world of descending water, and look at it. When I saw how much of it there was, and how fearfully in earnest it was, I was sorry I had gone behind it."

He goes on to tell the tale of his search for the peaceful Indians across Luna Island and to Terrapin Tower, and each time he comes across a lad or maiden who happens to have an Irish accent, and treats him badly for his questions about their culture. When he comes across a group of people and gives them a degrading "welcoming" speech, the people attack him and throw him over the falls:

"It was the quickest operation that ever was. I simply saw a sudden flash in the air of clubs, brick- bats, fists, bead-baskets, and moccasins- a single flash, and they all appeared to hit me at once, and no two of them in the same place. In the next instant the entire tribe was upon me. They tore half the clothes off me; they broke my arms and legs; they gave me a thump that dented the top of my head till it would hold coffee like a saucer; and, to crown their disgraceful proceedings and add insult to injury, they threw me over the Niagara Falls, and I got wet.

"About ninety or a hundred feet from the top, the remains of my vest caught on a projecting rock, and I was almost drowned before I could get loose. I finally fell, and brought up in a world of white foam at the foot of the Fall, whose celled and bubbly masses towered up several inches above my head. Of course I got into the eddy. I sailed round and round in it forty-four times- chasing a chip and gaining on it- each round trip a half mile- reaching for the same bush on the bank forty-four times, and just exactly missing it by a hair's-breadth every time.

"At last a man walked down and sat down close to that bush, and put a pipe in his mouth, and lit a match, and followed me with one eye and kept the other on the match, while he sheltered it in his hands from the wind. Presently a puff of wind blew it out. The next time I swept around he said:

"Got a match?" "Yes; in my other vest. Help me out, please." "Not for Joe." When I came round again, I said:

"Excuse the seemingly impertinent curiosity of a drowning man, but will you explain this singular conduct of yours?"

"With pleasure. I am the coroner. Don't hurry on my account. I can wait for you. But I wish I had a match."

I said: "Take my place, and I'll go and get you one.

He declined. This lack of confidence on his part created a coldness between us, and from that time forward I avoided him. It was my idea, in case anything happened to me, to so time the occurrence as to throw my custom into the hands of the opposition coroner over on the American side. At last a policeman came along, and arrested me for disturbing the peace by yelling at people on shore for help. The judge fined me, but I had the advantage of him. My money was with my pantaloons and my pantaloons were with the Indians. "When he asked a doctor where the horrible tribe of Indians were from, the doctor answered, 'Limerick, my son.'" (www.4literature.net/Mark_Twain/Niagara/)

Mark Twain's humorous account of the area in and around the falls also addresses the power and destruction, death and danger, and the changes in the world at that time.

The Falls have a secret calling, and those who answer the call are never disappointed. For some that means the temptation to perform stunts and gain recognition as a daredevil. Some have come to Niagara Region to fight in wars, and whether or not they were victorious, some of those people stayed even after their deaths. Some people simply come to the Falls to die. Over the years there have been many counts of heroism, successful stunts, and miraculous events. I'd like to share the darker side of the falls with you. These are the stories behind the spirits that time left behind, the people who have died and the possible sacrifices to Tawiscara, the evil god of Niagara.

Part One

Spirits

Do YOU Believe?

You saw a... what? A ghost? Have you lost your mind? Skeptics might never believe you. True believers, however, will hang on your every word. Some people would argue that the world is losing its sense of religion, or that some people are getting lost in what they believe to be religion. To believe in something means that we trust or have faith in something to be true, or to accept a story. To have a strong belief in something means that we have a conviction that something we are told is, in fact, true. Do you believe that ghosts can exist when told a credible enough story, or do you have a strong belief that they are real no matter what anyone says? Are you a skeptic? We live in a largely scientific world where everything has to be proven and documented before we give it any credence. Before embarking on our journey to Niagara, let's take a look at both sides of the paranormal argument, and open our minds to what the believers and the skeptics have to say.

There are different kinds of ghosts, or spirits that have been defined over the years. To help us learn a little bit more about what we're dealing with, Adam Woog wrote in his book, *Poltergeists*, that there are several categories of apparitions. There are the people who have an out-of-body experience where living people are able to appear in far away places (to be with loved ones before they die) and they are carried through very strong emotional desires. The most commonly reported ghosts are the ones who stay in specific places for very long periods of time, just as you would find in a famous haunted house. Another group consists of the "crisis apparitions" or those that have died and are sticking around this world to either send a very important message, or to take care of specific matters before they move along to the next world. This only happens once, generally. The fourth category Woog describes, and what many of us are most afraid of, is poltergeists.

"Poltergeists, then, are apparitions that make noise or that move, lift, or throw objects around. Unlike other types of ghosts, poltergeists are not visible; nor can they converse with the living. Poltergeists make themselves known by creating noise or throwing objects around. (*Poltergeists*, 12-13) Later in the book he expands a little more to mention that a poltergeist can produce odd and terrifying effects like "blood oozing from pictures that hang on the walls." More commonly they just move furniture around, make strange noises, pull on bed sheets, and play with the lights. Unlike regular hauntings that happen at night, poltergeists can happen by day as well. In some cases, humans have been hurt or held down, been bitten or kissed. Typically, a poltergeist only sticks around for about three weeks.

Similarly, Paranormal Scientist Hans Holzer categorizes paranormal phenomena in *Ghosts* (the encyclopedia) into three types excluding poltergeists:

1. A bona fide ghost – that is, a person who has passed out of the physical body but remains in the etheric body (aura, soul) at or near the place of the passing due to emotional ties or trauma. Such entities are people in trouble, who are seeking to understand their predicament and are usually not aware of their own passing.

2. No more than 10-15% of all sightings or other phenomena are 'real' ghosts. The larger portion of all sightings or sound phenomena is caused by a replaying of a past emotional event, one that has somehow been left behind, impressed into the atmosphere of the place or house... they occur exactly in the same place and at the same time of day to all those who witness them. These phenomena are called psychic impressions, and they are in a way like photographs of past events, usually those with high emotional connotations.

3. There are cases in which sightings or sounds of this kind are caused by the living who are far away, not in time but geographically. 'Phantoms of the living' is one name given the phenomenon, which is essentially telepathic. Usually these apparitions or sounds occur when it is urgent that a person reach someone at a distance... These projections of the inner body are involuntary, and cannot be controlled. A variant of these phenomena, however, deliberate projections, which occur when a person puts all their emotional strength into meeting someone who is far away. Instances of this are quite rare, however.

In some cases, spirits are defined as the part of us that separates from our bodies after we die and move on to the next world, perhaps after a quick stop to let loved ones know that we're okay, or to give a message. Ghosts, on the other hand, stick around. They are emotional impressions, or the occasional soul that just can't figure out what happened or where to go next. Most people use the two terms interchangeably. Holzer also mentions that ghosts and spirits cannot hurt you. The only thing to fear is fear itself and people have hurt themselves either by accident or subconsciously when they think they've seen a ghost.

Of course, he was not talking about poltergeists.

There are many tools that can be used to track down ghosts and try to record these events. Some people have even seen odd shapes and maybe even faces show up in their own photographs. Between cameras, infrared, thermographic tools, microphones, the list of possible scientific tools to track the paranormal is long. Almost as long as the number of dowsing or psychic tools such as the infamous Ouija board, tarot cards, crystal balls, mediums and so forth. Unfortunately, our ghostly friends can be quite elusive. They show up when the cameras are off, or they disappear when a stranger shows up to witness an event. If we do catch them, it's only once and that is a far cry from scientific evidence of their existence.

When researching this book, I knew I was not going to be using any "tools," scientific or psychic, to prove any stories for not only this reason, but because you would also have to believe in the accuracy of each tool used. I have no microphone recordings and, although I took pictures, I was not intending to see anything in them besides the subject of the photo. I'm not a paranormal researcher that investigates the funny sounds in your attic, I am not a psychic that sees messages for you in a crystal ball, and I am not Bill Murray from "Ghostbusters." (But what a fun movie that was!) I am a skeptical believer. I am aware of the effects of wind or old wood in a building making strange noises, I know that things moving when we don't expect them to can usually be explained, and I've met my share of fakes and hoaxes that wanted my money. But I believe that there is a part of us that exists and moves on after we die. I believe it's possible for energies (or ghosts) to get stuck here or decide to stay here, but I need proof. I'm a spiritual person in the new millennium.

Harry Houdini desperately wanted to believe in ghosts and the ability to communicate with them especially after his mother died, but he could not find any proof. He put out a challenge to anyone who could report or show him something that he could not reproduce. Everything from levitating phones, moving furniture, and disappearing items, he was able to mimic each and every single occurrence using magic tricks. He desperately wanted proof, but it had to be an absolute and unquestionable truth, not a person's belief. Over the centuries there have been many stories of frauds, hoaxes, and so called psychics who are out to dupe the public and take their money, or just to get attention before they were discovered to be fakes. (Perhaps John Edward from "Crossing Over" comes to mind?)

Harry Houdini was not the only famous skeptic. Another famous man, and to some he's considered the enemy of parapsychology, is James Randi, co-founder of the Committee for Scientific Investigation of Claims of the Paranormal (CSICOP). He published *Flim-Flam!* in 1980, and in 1989 he had his own investigatory TV program called, "Exploring Psychic Powers: Live!" where there was a prize of $100,000,000 dollars for the first person to offer real proof of paranormal phenomenon. The show did not last long as one psychic after another failed to prove anything, and the show became boring to watch when nothing paranormal happened. "Science is, quite simply, a search for knowledge of the universe around us. We observe, we draw conclusions from those observations, we design experiments to examine those conclusions, and we end up stating a theory which should express a new fact or idea. But, if new or better evidence comes along, we must either discard our theory or amend it to accommodate that evidence." (*James Randi: Psychic Investigator*, 15)

Randi admits that scientists are not always right and can make mistakes, but after some trial and error the same experiments can be carried out today as they were a hundred years ago and still show the same results. This is what he's after — this repeatable proof that anyone can do these tests and come up with the same results at any time. Randi can also perform magic tricks, slight of hand and other methods, that are commonly used by others as proof of the paranormal, and he shows them off during his lectures. Of course, there are many people who would like nothing better than to stop him in his tracks and discredit Randi, but, "It is a fact that no paranormal, psychic or supernatural claim has ever been substantiated by proper testing. It's not enough to merely gather huge amounts of anecdotal material in support of these avowed powers, and correct testing methods are not always seen to be so" (*James Randi: Psychic Investigator*, 19).

So, why do I still believe? Perhaps it's because the human race has always needed to know if we have a soul, or if there is something waiting for us after death. Maybe it's just something that scientific methods cannot measure? It might be beyond what we know how to measure, or the tools are not available to us yet. Possibly someone in the next generation will invent something that will undoubtedly prove the existence of ghosts.

One more thing I'd like to consider on a scientific scale, is the chance that the person experiencing and reporting ghostly sightings could have a different kind of... source. Hallucinations are not just for the people that we perceive to be crazy or schizophrenic. We have to consider certain psychological possibilities. People who are not in any way affected by mental illness can still have regular hallucinations. Stress alone can increase the likeliness of these hallucinations, and naturally so can the lack of sleep, or use of drugs or alcohol. "More than seventy percent of a sample of 375 college students had at some time experienced an auditory hallucination of hearing voices while they were awake. Such hallucinations may readily be mistaken for ghosts or taken as evidence of the paranormal by those experiencing them. This is especially true since the high frequency of these waking hallucinations is not a well-known finding." (*Pseudoscience and the Paranormal*, 61)

Maybe that's why people are reluctant to talk about their ghostly sightings. Perhaps people are afraid that they will come across as sounding crazy if they talk about the things that go bump in the night? You might be an adamant or secret believer, you might be skeptical, or you might just be curious. You can make your own conclusions after reading the following stories.

The Olde Angel Inn

224 Regent Street
Niagara-on-the-Lake
www.angel-inn.com

View of the Olde Angel Inn from Regent Street.

I t's no secret — the Olde Angel Inn is haunted. They're not trying to hide it. The staff wants you to know about it ... so that you can come and meet the good Captain yourself.

Captain Colin Swayze served with the British-Canadian forces during the War of 1812 and is said to walk the halls of the Inn late at night, and occasionally rattle the dishes in the kitchen or pile up the silverware after the tables have been set. As long as the British Flag hangs over the front door of the Inn, Captain Swayze remains perfectly harmless.

Back in 1789 the building was built as the Harmonious Coach House. After the American retreat, the structure was burnt down. It was rebuilt again after the war in 1815 by John Ross, and he named it the Olde Angel Inn. During the late 1800s, the name was changed to The Mansion House, then to Fraser's Hotel, and then back to the Olde Angel Inn. The English style pub on the main floor runs in the same manner as it did back in 1812 and it consists of a restaurant, the pub area, and a Snug room (from the custom of having a room reserved for patrons who do not want to be seen in a public bar).

Newspaper clippings from the 1820s include reports of footsteps from the darkened dining room, the clinking of glasses, laughter, conversation, and the rearranging of table settings, all of which the owners were well aware. Florence Le Doux passed away towards the end of the 1990s, but she told stories about Captain Swayze as much as she could before passing. Florence had claimed that her own abilities to play piano, draw, and sculpt were handed down to her directly from the Captain's generous, ghostly instruction.

I was fortunate enough to stumble across a book by the professional psychic from Quebec, Najla Mady, called, *BOO! Ghosts I Have(n't) Loved*. There are two chapters about her ghostly adventures in Niagara-on-the-Lake, and the first of the two talks about Captain Swayze and the Olde Angel Inn, "The Captivating Captain." Najla recounts the story about Florence Le Doux, who shared over seventy years with the ghost, and whose great-grandfather met the living Captain

Swayze when he bought the Inn. They researched Swayze's family tree and wrote to relatives in England. They sent the portrait of Swayze and told them about his talents in painting, sculpting, and playing the piano. The crew that was with Najla rushed to set up all of their equipment to record her psychic impressions as she walked through the Inn.

"My instincts directed me to the far left corner of the building. While approaching the area, I felt overcome by a sense of suffering. The feeling intensified as I drew closer. Suddenly, I realized that what I was picking up was coming not from the room, but from below the floorboards on which I was standing. I felt pain, unnatural pain, caused by torture. Beatings, broken bones, starvation, bloodshed – I felt it all. I also felt the small area wasn't a part of the rest of the Inn. It was different somehow.

"My eyes were drawn to a portrait of George Washington hanging on the wall in this particular area. The thought that flew through my mind was it definitely shouldn't be there. I also noticed a portrait of a British officer. As I gazed at the painting I saw the silhouette of two more officers. This told me that all three had suffered the same tortuous fate.

"I expressed my thoughts and feelings to the camera before moving onto other areas of the building. I was drawn to one particular bedroom upstairs. I learned later that this was the room Florence had been born in. I turned to a hotel employee and remarked that this was truly a very busy room. I could hear fife and drum music, soldiers were marching and there were beautifully dressed young ladies and gentlemen in army uniforms strolling arm in arm." (*BOO!*, 62)

The employee working there at the time told Najla that she was not the only one to hear music coming from that room, and that some of the staff had suspected that there might have been more than one presence living there.

Najla also went to visit Florence Le Doux to talk to her further about her personal relationship with the Captain:

"Pointing to a portrait of Swayze, she told us that she painted it while his hands guided hers. A well-executed bust of the talented ghost sits proudly on display. Florence tells us Swayze actually molded it using her hands and grey clay she picked up from nearby Fort Mississauga. He told her what type of clay to use and where she'd find it. Florence often treated patrons of the Angel Inn to an impromptu piano serenade. She happily told us that it was Swayze who taught her to play the instrument." (*Boo!*, 63)

Florence Le Doux had to explain the ghosts to hundreds of people and she didn't mind openly discussing the strange events and sightings. She alone had counted about eighty women who told her about a man in a red uniform standing behind them in the ladies public bathroom in the basement. She said the spirits have also entered the bedrooms of overnight guests. Once, while she was talking to another psychic, an employee who walked into the room told them that he did not believe in the paranormal. The psychic called out to Captain Swayze and challenged him, asking if he was going to allow being spoken to in such a manner. A heavy mug flew across the room. It brushed against the waiter's hand, cutting it and making it bleed, before hitting one of the oak support beams. The waiter confessed that he believed, and the dent the mug left is still there to this day.

Not all of the ghost stories are old. More recently, one of the owners awoke to a hammering outside his bedroom. He got up only to find that the heavy horseshoe he'd nailed to a post had been flung onto the floor, but not directly down to the floor below where it was hung, it was a full twenty feet away. There was nobody around. Captain Swayze also doesn't like when the staff members argue, and he will throw dishes across the room when two people are confronting each other. On the right night, you can listen to live music while you sit in the bar with some friends and your favourite beers. Keep in mind when you order your drink that Swayze likes to disrupt the kegs of American beer, he's known to be still holding a grudge against Americans to this day.

No matter what you're drinking, eventually ladies, you will have to use the bathroom. That is the location where Captain Swayze died while hiding in a barrel before American bayonets took his life. Some women get a feeling like they are being watched while using the bathroom, others report being bumped while washing their hands at the sink, and some see him or his shadow in the mirror behind them before turning around to see that there's nobody in the room. (Do not mistake this for the short statue that can be found in the bathroom.) Not only was Swayze a talented artist and musician, he was a ladies' man.

Aside from the separate cottages available, some of the rooms are above or adjacent to the lively action of the main floor pub. After all the music has been played, the visiting patrons have left, and the staff cleans up, you might be able to settle in for a quiet night's sleep.

Or maybe not.

Some hotel guests still hear bangs coming from below at night, or heavy footsteps and male laughter, along with fife and drum music in the upstairs bedroom.

There are a number of different stories that could explain what might have led Captain Swayze to the Olde Angel Inn that fateful night, during the battle for Fort George. He could have been coming to visit his

Sneaking a picture in the ladies' room.

sweetheart, Euretta the barmaid, one last time. He could have been trying to stop the Americans from celebrating with English Rum. He could have wanted to take a rest from the fighting for a pint himself. Whatever the reason that brought him back, you will find the Union Jack over the front door to keep him happy. For the guests that dare to stay the whole night, they qualify for a Certificate of Survival.

Najla also writes that Florence had moved from the Inn and she claims that Captain Swayze moved with her, introducing himself to her granddaughter. Could that last part be true? Or is the Captain still at the Inn?

My first visit to the Inn was back in December of 2006. My husband Giasone (or "G") and I were there initially to meet up with a group of people for a Walking Ghost Tour hosted by Haunted Hamilton (www.hauntedhamilton.com). The tour started right after we grabbed a bite to eat in the

Pub. (You will find out about some of the stories we were told in the following sections in this book.) The tour also concluded at the Angel Inn, and we decided to warm up and relax while listening to some music before calling it a night. We would have liked to stay the night in the Captain's Room, but it's such a busy Inn our last minute plans left us at another nearby hotel in town. We enjoyed the Angel Inn Lager in the Snug room, and I noticed that the cast iron below some of the tables resembled (or were) old Singer sewing tables but without the moving pedals. We have visited since and each time we've enjoyed the food and drinks we've ordered. We were lucky enough to catch some fantastic live bands, and even if you're not looking for Captain Swayze, it's a great spot to hit if you're in Niagara-on-the-Lake.

(I did go down to the ladies' bathroom, alone. I didn't see or hear anything out of the ordinary. For those of you who have already been there I'll have you know, I did not lift the leaf.)

The Buttery

The Buttery
19 Queen, Niagara On The Lake
www.thebutteryrestaurant.com

The front entrance to The Buttery.

The ghosts that haunt The Buttery in Niagara-on-the-Lake were not left behind after the War of 1812. Passing by on the street, The Buttery looks like a charming and quaint restaurant and tavern. The pathway leads up to a heated porch area for outdoor eating and a great spot to watch Shaw theatre patrons walking by. The walls inside are lined with portraits of actors and productions from the past and it's a wonderful place to gather with friends for dinner or just a few drinks.

If you like to have a little extra company as well, The Buttery can offer a ghost or two to keep you entertained. There are a couple of outcomes to this story, so I'll tell you both versions. A husband had abused his wife for years, and in 1850, she conspired with her brother to murder him by pushing him down the stairs from the second story. She then buried him in the cellar. She is said to have died soon after, guilt weighing heavily upon her. One story says that she still haunts The Buttery by herself, but another version of the story includes the haunting by both her and her husband.

The Ontario Ghosts and Hauntings Research Society (www.torontoghosts.org) posted about this story online and received a response in February 2006 that continues the story in a different direction.

The kitchens and bathrooms are in the basement with two stairwells for access to the dining area on the main floor. There is only one stairwell going up to the second floor at the back of the building, where the husband must have been pushed. Reports of ghostly activity include the toilets in the women's bathroom flushing on their own, music starting on its own, the lights leading to the second story going out, and servers having trays knocked out of their hands.

Stranger still, a visitor from the Southern States had more of a story to tell. A self-proclaimed medium had stopped short in front of The Buttery when she felt incredibly strong vibrations and demanded to speak to the owners. After accurately describing the ghostly events that had taken place with the staff members, they agreed to a séance.

The results of that séance revealed a story about a doctor named Phillip, his wife, and handicapped son from the mid-nineteenth century. His wife's constant doting over the boy, and the embarrassment of being a doctor with a son that was ill, was too much for the doctor to bear. Besides, the boy could not appreciate her efforts and her duties as a wife were being neglected. One day, while she was in the kitchen preparing food for her son, he snuck upstairs and smothered him with a pillow. When his wife came up the stairs with a tray of soup and saw what he had done, she screamed. Phillip bounded out the door and in doing so, knocked the tray from her hands, the impact causing her to fall down the stairs to her death. Because he was a doctor, he was able to fill out the death certificates as he saw fit and without being questioned. After this séance, the spirits of the mother and son were freed, but Phillip remained. Occasionally, when strange things happen at The Buttery, the staff call out to him by name and ask him to stop. The occurrences were said to have slowed, and then eventually stopped.

I know that the Ontario Ghosts and Hauntings Research Society can only post what they are given on their website. The person who reported this heard the story that they were told directly from a veteran staff member who experienced this séance. However, this particular story of a doctor and wife taking care of a handicapped son is very close to a story I heard on a ghost tour while in New Orleans a few years ago. I wonder if the medium from the "Southern States" might have been from Louisiana. I don't know if there is a ghost at The Buttery. If so, it could be Phillip or the wife he abused that killed him, their handicapped son...or all three.

G and I went for lunch at The Buttery and it was very busy. We sat at a funky, hammered-bronze table and watched the staff keep up with the number of customers piling in. When I was able to steal a moment from our waitress, Kim,

I asked if there were any ghost stories she could tell me. Her face lit up and she told me she wished she had more time to sit and tell me about all of the strange things she'd seen and heard about while working there. She did invite me to "just walk around the building for a while and you'll find your own ghost stories!" I gave her my card and told her to get in touch with me when she had time.

I took her up on her offer and walked around as much as I could without getting in the way of the staff or other patrons. (I must have looked absolutely lost.) I didn't see the door leading upstairs, but I wasn't exactly able to stand still long enough or reach the back of the room to

The stairwell going down to the bathrooms at The Buttery.

really look carefully. I did make my way down the narrow stairwell to the bathrooms in the back, and came back up the second stairwell at the front of the restaurant.

Nothing happened to me or to my husband when he tried the same thing. As far as I could see, nobody emerged from the stairs looking like something odd had happened while we were there. Of course, these things happen randomly, and since the staff is there for so many hours each day they have a much greater chance of experiencing anything. I wasn't disappointed.

Cavendish Manor

5781 Dunn Street
Niagara Falls
www.cavendishmanor.com

S ometimes the ghosts are not as blatant, and they might not be as aggressive or playful as we might expect (or hope). There may be times when a quick glance or a simple giggle is all there is to experience, and not very often. Or so we hope.

The Cavendish Manor is a retirement home. This is not the type of residence where you would anticipate, and certainly not look forward to, a haunting of any kind. What you do hope to find is a comfortable and friendly atmosphere with quality care. That is precisely what this retirement home provides. Close to community activities and public transportation, the Cavendish Manor offers many services. I've still got a few more years before I can plan on living somewhere with a whirlpool, games room, multiple lounges, and a hair salon. Sigh…

This charming and safe area also has a history, much like the rest of the areas along the border. This tale, however, is not about the war or people killing each other in rage. There is a sad story behind the Cavendish Manor—the site of an old school with an attached swimming pool. Some little girls had drowned in that pool many years ago and now the residents at the Manor report a few sightings of their ghosts. Some have seen the girls running through the residence, most of the time in the back stairwell and kitchen lobby area.

Other reports include hearing the little girls giggling, and in some cases, their screams. Eventually, the people who kept hearing the girls' voices began to connect them to other events in the Manor as well. Some of the residents of Cavendish Manor believe that when the little girls are heard, someone will die soon after. I wondered if the girls' giggling could have possibly been someone else's grandchildren that had come to visit and ran away before they were seen. If it is a ghostly occurrence, is it really a message of death from the other side? Perhaps those are questions that will never be answered.

The Cavendish Manor is, after all, a warm and friendly place to spend your years of retirement. I wouldn't worry too much about little giggles in the background.

The Devil's Hole

The State Park website for the Devil's Hole is
http://nysparks.state.ny.us/parks/info.asp?parkID=28

Inside The Devil's Hole as seen from approximately one quarter of the
way down towards the water.

Long before the European settlers came in the
1700s, the Seneca Indians inhabited the land
around the Falls, which they considered to
be the home of deities known as the Great Spirit of
Thunder Waters, He-No the Thunderer, and Lelawala,
the Maid of the Mist. The area around Three Sisters
Islands (three small islands off the west side of Goat
Island) was the location of many sacrifices to the
gods, or spirits. About four miles down river is the

three hundred foot deep gorge called the Devil's Hole, also named by the Seneca Indians as they believed that it was the home of the "Evil One," who took the form of a giant snake. The Senecas warned travelers about the location, but not everyone listened to them. In 1687 the French explorer Robert de la Salle was murdered by the members of his own expedition in the Devil's Hole.

Almost a century later, the deaths continued in brutal fashion. For those not familiar with the Conspiracy of Pontiac, the Devil's Hole Massacre was one of the most brutal events recorded from that time. In 1755, Pontiac, an Indian Chief and leader of the Ottawa, Ojibwa and Potawatomi, was on his way to occupy Michilimackinac and other allied French

A view from the top of the Devil's Hole, where you can see trees that have blocked the view to the bottom.

Some of the winding and sloping steps in the Devil's Hole.

Forts. After meeting Major Rogers, he also allowed the English troops to pass untouched as long as they were shown respect by the British. By the time Pontiac and his men reached the Forts, he discovered that he was given empty promises by the French and they were no longer welcome in the area. The English also intruded and deprived them of their hunting grounds by building encroaching English settlements without telling them.

In 1763 the Indian "prophet" preached of a union of Indians to expel the English. Taking advantage of the religious fervour at the time, he organized a simultaneous attack on English forts, careful of planning it for a certain phase of the moon. About five hundred Senecas surprised a wagon train escorted by twenty-four English soldiers. They were ambushed and driven over the edge of the Devil's Hole. A party was sent from Fort Niagara to rescue them and they too, were nearly annihilated. In all, eighty scalped and otherwise mutilated bodies were recovered by the few rescuers who were sent in vain and were still alive. Horses and screaming victims were thrown into the gorge and the nearby stream, still known today as Bloody Run. (A few years later, Pontiac was killed in Cahokia, Illinois outside of St. Louis by an Indian who was bribed by an Englishman and a new, bitter war began with the Pontiac followers.)

In 1892 construction began on a railway that would allow the Great Gorge Trolley to take passengers back and forth from Queenston to Chippawa. Of course, this meant that the Trolley passed by the Devil's Hole every day. On July 1, 1917, twelve tourists died and twenty-four tourists were injured when a trolley filled with passengers derailed and plunged into the Niagara River at the upper end of the Whirlpool Rapids just below the Whirlpool Bridge. The cause of this tragic accident was a result of heavy rains undermining the rail bed. The trolley rolled down a thirty-foot embankment and came to rest upside down on several submerged rocks before rolling onto its side and into the raging river. On September 17, 1935 at 2 a.m., five thousand tons of rock fell approximately 150 feet north of the Whirlpool Bridge, destroying more than two hundred feet of track and rail bed. This was that largest rock fall to plague the Great Gorge Route. It forced the Great Gorge Route to close for business, and the line along the base of the Niagara Gorge on the American side was never repaired or reopened.

Over the years, many "accidents" have happened in and around the Devil's Hole. Some have been suicides, murders, and some were said to be "slip and fall" mishaps. Police have reported evidence of modern-day Satan-worshipping activity, perhaps taking advantage of the convenient name of the location.

Perhaps you should go and visit for yourself? The New York State Park's website invites you to the park for a relaxing afternoon: "Devil's Hole State Park overlooks the lower Whirlpool rapids. A wildly beautiful walkway leads down from the park along the turbulent Niagara River 300 feet into the wooded gorge and offers an up-close, spectacular view of the gorge's rapids. Devil's Hole has picnic areas, hiking, and nature trails. It is one of the most popular spots for fishermen."

G and I went to the Devil's Hole, which was very easy to find along the Moses Parkway in New York. As soon as I saw it, I was impressed. I also knew my entire afternoon was going to consist of going down and back up the stairs. Many, many stairs. They start out pretty even with a railing, but that doesn't last long. About half way down, I had to stop for a break. The steps are large uneven stones, and there's nothing to hold on to so you have to keep your balance. There were a lot of joggers and some young families that only went partway down. I didn't go down the very last fifty steps, but G told me they were the steepest of them all, and he was able to climb down by the water and take some pictures.

It was extremely beautiful. I was able to take breaks and sit on the rocks in the shade and make a couple of notes to the sound of the rushing water. When it was time to go back up, I knew I was going to have to make rest stops along the way—and I decided to count the steps. It's a rough number since I wasn't sure when to count jutting rocks or slopes as steps, but I counted three hundred and thirty, and add G's bottom forty or fifty to that total for an idea of the depth of the Devil's Hole. You might also find a sign pointing towards a Limestone Cave, which is supposed to be the home of the Evil Spirit. Unfortunately I was unable to climb over to see it myself. Once we were back up at the top and looking down, you can only see a fraction of the full distance, but I know that anyone who was pushed or fell over that edge could not survive.

A picture taken of the Niagara River from the bottom of the Devil's Hole.

Hawley-Breckenridge House

Mississauga Street
Niagara-on-the-Lake

The Hawley-Breckenridge house dates back to 1796 when it was built as two separate buildings. Renovations merged the two into the house that stands today. In the late 1800s, an officer of the British Army (who was also a veteran of India), Major Charles Stanley Herring, made it his home. The Hawley-Breckenridge house was one of the first buildings to be restored in Niagara-on-the-Lake and can be found on Mississauga Street.

"As a destination of the underground railroad, a number of freed slaves found their way through the house. Six of them are buried in the backyard" (http://hauntedontario. netfirms.com/notl.html).

On at least one occasion after 1899, Major Herring saw a woman in a long-grey dress that "disappeared like smoke." The woman appeared to be in her thirties, a tiny woman with long brown hair, wearing a bonnet and a long dress. Over the years people have named her Elizabeth, although we do not know what her original story was, or her real name.

According to John Robert Colombo's book, *Mysterious Canada*, Mr. and Mrs. Hawley purchased the home in 1953. They did not know about any ghostly appearances before they took over the house. However, they too experienced strange knockings and banging. Nothing that was harmful happened to them and it was hardly a disturbance—the Hawleys just got used to having Elizabeth around. Sometimes even guests of the Hawleys reported seeing the apparition of a young girl on the main floor of the home.

When they invited a psychic to the house, she spotted the ghost and said she "felt" that the ghost was that of a woman who died in the house in the mid-1800s after spending much of her life devoted to caring for her infirmed parents. There have also been updates and new sightings as the years have progressed.

In the *St. Catherine's Standard* newspaper in 1982, an article by Michael Clarkson gave this information from the Hawleys: "She walks or stands for a few seconds, then disappears; but it's not a frightening experience. It's just as if she's checking to see if everything's okay."

Author Kyle Upton writes in *Niagara's Ghosts 2* in 2004: "This petite, brown haired woman is seen on the stairs, and sometimes makes her way out the front comes downstairs and exists through the front door."

Obviously, Elizabeth likes it in the Hawley-Breckenridge house and has no intention of leaving. It is common to hear the brass knocker on the front door being used, along with raps on the back door only to find out that nobody is standing there. She has never harmed anyone, and doesn't go out of her way to interfere or scare any visitors in the home.

However, one story on the Haunted Ontario website (http://hauntedontario.netfirms.com) mentions that… "Doors have been known to crash and bang when unwelcome guests are present."

Najla Mady, the professional psychic from Quebec, also went to the Hawley-Breckenridge house to talk to Frank Hawley after she finished visiting the Olde Angel Inn. Frank told her that he'd met the former owner of the house and had made a joke about not being told about the ghosts that came along with the purchase. The owner purposely didn't say anything in order to make the sale and moved out. A noted historian and steam engine inventor, Frank was not exactly whimsical about the situation, but let Najla and her crew in to tape the television show.

In the first room that they entered, Najla saw a very large brick fireplace that was large enough to fit a large-sized pot over the fire, and still had the wrought iron handle that held the cooking utensils. Frank was a busy man, and while he was busy on the phone, they took it upon themselves to finish touring the house on their own. Najla felt vibrations all over the place, the upper and lower levels, as well as the coach house located next to the house.

> "The coach house was now used for the servant's quarters and stood vacant. I picked up the spirit of a man living there, dressed in clothing of days passed. I said that he had recently moved an object in one of the rooms.
> "Entering the formal living room, I saw a young boy and girl beautifully dressed in velvet and lace and quietly amusing themselves. There was a sense of reserve about them and I felt them to be ill – lung problems most likely. Then the scene changed and I saw a young woman in her mid-twenties. I felt her to be mischievous, moving articles here and there, now and again." (*Boo!*, 67)

Najla also sensed that there had been knocking on the back door of the house. The host of the television show informed her that Frank had often gone running for the back door to answer a knocking, only to find nobody there, and in the winter there were no footprints.

> "I felt that the dominant spirit of the house was a Civil War soldier. I saw a man of large build, stubborn, and not eager to leave what he felt was his home. He wanted to be master of the house and was antagonistic toward Frank. It was he who kept Frank running to answer his repetitious knocking..."

They joined back up with Frank in the room with the fireplace when they finished their own tour of the house. That room had been the scullery house where the cooking was done, separate from the main house. (It was uncivilized back then to have cooking smells wafting through the house and servants delivered the food to the main dining room.)

> "... Frank and several others have seen an apparition of a young woman appearing to be in her mid-twenties in that room. She would observe them, wrapped in a mist before slowly disappearing.
>
> "After we finished our interview for the television camera, I asked Frank if I could see the interior of the coach house. Since he had been on the phone when I discussed the moved object, he was unaware of the reason I wanted to view it. When I explained the reason, he seemed surprised, saying that he had been in the apartment the previous day and all had been in order. However, he readily agreed to let me see the coach house.
>
> "We entered a beautifully furnished apartment. At first glance everything looked to be in order. Under closer scrutiny I saw the moved object. I pointed to a small table where an empty candle holder was sitting. Beside the holder lay the candle. Pointing to the candle, I said that it had been taken out of its holder. Frank appeared puzzled. He had seen the short candle sitting in its deep holder the previous day."
> (*Boo!*, 68-69)

The skeptic in me wonders how that candle fell out of the holder. I don't know if there are any breezes that are strong enough on a windy day to knock it over. Could a small animal have gotten in and bumped it? Maybe Frank saw the fallen candle the day before, meant to fix it and didn't, and under Najla's suggestion swears that it was previously upright? I'm more likely to believe when people tell me they've seen a woman in her twenties disappear, or if there's a distinct knock on a door and nobody there with no footprints in the snow. This precarious circumstance with the candle doesn't rule out all other possible factors, which I think is essential in these types of "physical proof" situations.

Lundy's Lane

http://www.battleoflundyslane.com/

"Brave rifles, veterans, you have been baptized in fire and blood and have come out steel!"

— *Winfield Scott*

The Lundy's Lane monument and cannons in the Drummond Hill Cemetery

During the War of 1812, the 6'5" General Winfield Scott led his American troops from Buffalo to a series of attacks on the British and Canadian forces on the Canadian side of the border. During the Battle of Queenston Heights (near Niagara-on-the-Lake) Scott was captured and held as a Prisoner of War. When he was released, Scott reunited with his friend, Captain John Wool, and returned to duty to continue fighting in the area.

On July 25, 1814, General Winfield Scott advanced uphill towards where the British held ground. They were greeted by a few headstones that were side by side with the artillery that guarded the surrounding areas of Niagara Falls. The British were under the command of Lieutenant General Gordon Drummond, who was able to completely ambush Scott and his men when they arrived by hiding along a dusty cart track bordered by trees and grassy perimeter. Rather than retreating, Scott decided to make an advance instead to make the British believe that he had a much larger army with him. The Americans were bayoneting the British in the dark as they tried to reload, but instead of retreating themselves, the British had more troops arrive to back them up.

The night sky, the smoke and gun powder clouds, and being in the heat of battle, it was difficult for anyone to know whose men were on which side of the fight. Soldiers of the same army killed each other and enemies could walk past without being seen. Cannons fired, musket flares were seen from all directions, and the sounds of death multiplied quickly. For more than six hours, 1,300 men in Scott's command fought against contemptuous fire from the British. Although Captain John Wool was able to capture a redan gun from the British and burn down a nearby town of Bridgewater Mills (present-day Dufferin Islands), the British were able to capture two of the American cannons. With the score even, less than four hundred men were still alive when more troops came to back up Scott and Wool.

Scott withdrew and reorganized his men. While looking for a new place to attack, he was hit with a bullet, shattering a bone. Over 1,700 bodies littered the field, either dead or dying as surgeons tried to saw off limbs to save them. The British were left to clean up the battlefield and dug pits or burned the bodies, and scattered or buried the ashes. The Battle of Lundy's Lane, Canada's bloodiest battle, ended in a draw. Veterans of the war would tell the story to those that came to see the field and cemetery that

their own side won. The victory story you heard depended on who you asked.

Drummond Hill Cemetery is on Lundy's Lane, which runs through Niagara Falls. You will also be able to find the graves of British and American soldiers from the battle in 1841, as well as the grave of Laura Secord (some say the sculpture has eyes that follow you).

The area of the Cemetery itself was part of the battlefield and there have been sightings of five old Royal Scot soldiers limping across the field before disappearing. Three British soldiers have been seen pushing their way up the hill and then marching into battle. Others report that just being in the cemetery gives off a feeling of being in the wrong place, or an eerie notion of someone

Opposite: The front gates at the Drummond Hill Cemetery.
Above: Laura Secord's grave in the Drummond Hill Cemetery.

watching them. As the city grows, it continues to spread and build over the battlefield, turning up gruesome remnants of the battle. Attempts are being made by the Canada Millennium Partnership Project to preserve what's left of that land. (See http://www. battleoflundyslane.com for more information.)

Some nights, the red-coated soldiers can be seen climbing the hill toward the cemetery and passing by the houses. They could be spirits that fought alongside General Winfield Scott and Captain John Wool on that fateful night, or one of Drummond's men. If you were to visit Drummond Hill Cemetery today and take pictures, what do you think will show up? Simple orbs, or soldiers at war? What kind of energy does the bloodiest battle in Canada leave behind?

The Drummond Hill Cemetery, and Lundy's Lane Battlefield where soldiers are laid to rest, many with unmarked graves.

The grave of Lieutenant General Gordon Drummond.

McFarland House

15927 Niagara Parkway,
2 km south of Niagara-on-the-Lake,
in beautiful McFarland Point Park
www.niagaraparks.com/heritage/mcfarland.php
www.tourniagara.com/attractions/historical-sites/
mcfarland-house/

C ome to enjoy an authentic English Herb Tea Garden. Relax, have some tea, and treat yourself to a scone or two. Sit and chat with a friend as you wait for the guided tour through the McFarland House. The staff members are dressed in period clothing, waiting to tell you the story of John McFarland and his family.

John McFarland was a widower who came to Canada from Paisley, Scotland around 1782 with his four sons. Soon after arriving, John married his neighbour, Margaret Wilson, and their family grew with her additional five children. Working as a brick layer and carpenter, he steadily built his reputation and wealth enough to build a large house. He and his sons built the house in 1800 on land that was granted to them by King George III, using the bricks they made in their own kiln on the property. Their home was impeccably decorated with a lovely piano, crystal ceiling lights, and other status symbols and family heirlooms. Sadly, Margaret passed away in 1809. But that was just the beginning of the harrowing story for the old McFarland house.

During the War of 1812, the Americans asked John to give up his house to them. After refusing the soldiers, he was taken prisoner and sent to Greenbush, New York for the duration of the war. While he was gone his sons joined the British/Canadian militia, including the eleven-year old who worked as a "powder monkey," delivering gun powder to the soldiers manning the artillery during battle on the fields.

The house was used as a headquarters for British officers, as the location of British and American Artillery battalions protecting the Niagara River, and as a field hospital for American and British military. Many soldiers were carried in from battle badly wounded and, although some were saved, many died in the house and were buried around the property and near the river.

Strategically, the British built a gun emplacement behind the house to protect the town called Newark and the nearby river. With both American and British sides using the house, little respect was shown for the integrity of the structure. Americans destroyed bits of the building to burn and use as fuel. When John finally came back, his house was badly damaged, with windows, doors and mantels missing.

John McFarlane died in 1816, and as inscribed on his tombstone in St. Mark's Church, this list of atrocities contributed to his death. His sons rebuilt the home with love and for generations to come the McFarland family continued to live in the house for another 150 years. In 1959 the house was carefully restored once again and is furnished in the Empire period of pre-1840.

As you enter though a small kitchen and gift shop and take a tour though the McFarland house, imagine John and his sons making the bricks to make the house where you stand. Perhaps, if you listen closely enough while on the first floor, you might be able to catch a few hushed voices. Possibly the voices of his sons from so many generations ago that passed the house along to their next of kin. They could also be the voices of doctors who had worked in the hospital, or the last whispers of the soldiers who experienced a slow and painful death. Some people have heard footsteps in the lower part of the original house, thinking that other visitors were still there. Perhaps John still sadly walks around his house as he did in his last few days, missing his wife, and mourning over his beautiful home.

Enjoy your tea, have a delicious scone and chat with your friend before the tour. Just don't talk too loudly if you want to overhear someone or something else in the house with you.

Mr. Cale of Stamford, Ontario

It's hard to say where Mr. Cale's log home once stood in Stamford, a township on the outskirts of Niagara Falls, Ontario. Over the years so many developments have swept across the area, one can't say for sure exactly where Mr. Cale was located.

It might not even be a real story. It's hard to say when the tale is based on one report in the *Niagara Falls Evening Journal* on March 4, 1872. Apparently, somebody saw a ghost at the railroad crossing in Stamford Township.

Mr. Cale was described by a German woman as a "Negro" wearing the same kind of clothes as if he was on earth and barefoot. There are further descriptions of Mr. Cale that include a haggard expression, and "flaming eyes." That must have been one scary encounter! The tracks they spoke of were called the Great Western Railroad at the time.

The German woman saw him walking barefoot from the train crossing back to his log home, and then back across Mr. Berryman's fields. The distance was about a half mile, and even Mr. Berryman saw him enough times to give a similar description of Mr. Cale.

But, can a ghost leave footprints? Surely nobody in their right mind would go walking through the snow barefoot for ten feet, let alone a half mile! It's not like there are any animals that leave prints that could be mistaken for human feet in the Niagara Falls area. Even if two people at different times were imagining the same ghost, descriptions of footprints in the snow are a different matter completely.

People in the area speculated as to why Mr. Cale still walked his path from the tracks and across the field after death. It was possible that he was killed, perhaps in an accident at the train tracks? He could have been murdered or badly wounded and tried to reach the tracks to find people to help him. The original article suggested that Mr. Cale was not resting in peace because his affairs were not looked after post-mortem. He might have come back to right something that had gone wrong, or to take care of matters before moving on.

There is a railroad that runs through Stamford today. The Great Western Railroad is now the Canadian National Railroad, which still uses those tracks that Mr. Cale visited. Or still visits? Do you think you could find where the field was? You might see Mr. Cale heading towards where his log cabin home once was.

This kind of ghost story is my personal favourite. The only "evidence" is from a newspaper so long ago... it could have been a fun story on a slow news day and we'd never know. The lack of hardcore facts and photos leave us wondering if there ever was a Mr. Cale. We don't know where along the tracks he walked, and now surrounded by a golf course or park, any of those areas could have been Mr. Berryman's field. Part of the enjoyment and wonder of a good ghost story is not having any facts to shatter anything you might want to believe. Sometimes the idea is more enchanting than the history. In this case, the image of bare footprints in the snow is one that stays with you, and might even make you go looking for footprints yourself one day.

Niagara Falls Spirella Factory/Museum/Aviary

Niagara Falls Aviary,
5651 River Road,
Niagara Falls, Ontario
www.niagarafallslive.com/Aviary/

This story twists back and forth over the border, so instead of following the people, I'm going to follow the timeline as much as I can.

In 1827, the Niagara Falls Museum was founded by Thomas Barnett at the present site of the Queen Victoria Park Restaurant. The Museum was the oldest and largest of all private museums. Despite its impressive history and size, nothing could stop the changes that were about to be made to the property with the passing of the Niagara Falls Queen Victoria Parks Act in 1887. All of the land along the Niagara River from Clifton Hill to Dufferin Islands was expropriated, or taken away from the owners. Mr. Barnett had to find a new home for his Museum in Niagara Falls, New York, where he built a similar building called the Museum Arcade.

Meanwhile, on the Canadian side of the border, the Spirella Corset Company built a four-story concrete building in 1908. This corset manufacturing facility once employed 250 women.

I decided to take a peek into the background of the Spirella Factory. I'd like to introduce you to a few people who worked there...

• Elizabeth Isabella Combe was born in Hedley on the Hill near Newcastle in England on September 15, 1905, and came to Canada in 1807 when she was a year and a half old. Around 1920, Elizabeth went to work as a domestic and later was employed by the Spirella Corset Company. During World War I she worked for Bell Aircraft and was a cosmetologist in the 1950s before moving to California. After her husband died, she returned to Niagara Falls to live in a retirement home. The family history (incorrectly) tracked the retirement home to be the old Spirella building in 2002, where she died on May 2nd.

• Frances Violet worked in the Spirella Corset Factory in Niagara Falls, and afterwards in downtown Akron, Ohio, at O'Neils Department store in the Luggage Department.

• Meet the President: *Niagara Falls Journal*, Sept. 24, 1892: PERFECT FRUITS, VEGETABLES ARE PRODUCED ON FARM BEGUN AS HOBBY BY NIAGARA SPIRELLA EXECUTIVE

"W. W. Kincaid's Farm, Near Youngstown, Now Embraces Large Area and Is Model Establishment with Latest Devices for Cleanliness, Ease of Operation and Good Crops. Cantaloupes so large that a single man would have a difficult time consuming one at a sitting, water melons the reverse to size but of a deliciousness of meat which makes them a dainty for a queen, eggplant, asparagus and other vegetables and fruits of nearly every conceivable variety; things like these can be found on the farm of William W. Kincaid, president of the Spirella Company of this city. The farm is located on the River Road just as one enters the village of Youngstown. It is a truly marvellous establishment."

Everyone worked hard at the factory, and the people living in the area did well during the time when the clothes they were making were in high fashion. It was also a time that changed quickly when the industrial revolution took hold of the world. Business started to decline and many of the workers moved on, leaving only thirty employees. The Spirella Company had to move to a smaller location on Lewis Avenue in 1958.

Back over the border and looking at the Museum once again, we meet Jacob Sherman. In 1942, Mr. Sherman bought the Niagara Falls Museum from Thomas Barnett. It wasn't long before history repeated itself. The land where the museum was located was once again expropriated by the New York State government for the expansion of the State Reservation Park. He had no choice but to pick up everything (700,000 artifacts and over 2,000 photographs) and move the Museum once again over the border to Canada. Jacob Sherman bought the Spirella building and started major renovations to include a five-story viewing tower.

The Sherman family operated the museum until it was too expensive to maintain. In 1999, most of the contents and artifacts of the museum were sold to Bill Jamieson in Toronto, a private collector. He further sold many of the items including an Egyptian collection with mummies, and returned the remains of Ramses I to Egypt in 2003. (Of course, mummies belong in a different book, don't they?)

Larry Van, a Niagara-on-the-Lake resident, bought the building and again started renovations. A large addition was built on the south side of the building, and $15 million dollars later, the Niagara Falls Aviary opened in June

2003. The Aviary features three hundred tropical birds from around the world as well as an authentic wooden Java House, hand carved in Indonesia in 1875.

There have been strange sightings at the Aviary. "There are rumours of a friendly ghost who tidies up and appears in the uniform of a night watchman wandering the floors in the old part of the building." (Niagara Falls Public Library's website) But, who could it be? There have been so many people moving in and out of the building, and so many renovations. What is more likely? There could have been an accident during some of the renovations and the uniform of a foreman could be mistaken for a night watchman. It could have been someone working there at the Spirella Factory, a custodian. I wonder if Elizabeth Combe or Frances Violet worked with this man, if they knew him and said goodnight, as they ended their day and he began his night shift.

I have to be honest with you, dear reader. *ANY* birds found inside totally freak me out. I don't know why I have this crazy fear, but flying things inside building walls is just something I don't handle well. (Okay, I hide under my jacket and run screaming like a baby.) This is not something I'm going to investigate myself, but I'd like the rest of you to go and see for me! Let me know if you find this man walking along the old part of the building, making sure everything is in the right place, neat and tidy.

From the Aviary's website: "We invite you to celebrate birds with us and join us on an adventure that will have you imagine you have been transported back in time on an expedition in search of a mysterious legendary kingdom."

Oban Inn and Spa

160 Front Street
Niagara-on-the-Lake
http://www.obaninn.ca/

The entrance of the Oban Inn on Front Street.

I n 1824 Captain Duncan Mallory of Oban, Scotland built his home in Niagara-on-the-Lake where the Oban Inn now stands by the golf course. Even after the Captain passed away, people have heard him walking along the hallways or stomping around on the upper floor. But he's never been seen.

Outside the building, a woman has been seen standing around. She's been described as a "dishevelled old woman" wearing a white cook's outfit dating back to the early 1930s. Some people have seen her in the lower part of the Inn, but she's never made a sound.

A psychic once reported the definite presence of two distinct ghosts that occupied the building. There was a young woman who has been seen in the bathroom and another at the back stairs and entrance of the Inn.

The original building was completely destroyed by a fire on Christmas Day in 1992, leaving only the foundation. Miraculously one of the few things not destroyed by the fire was a painting of Captain Mallory's mother, which was completely unscathed. The building was reconstructed as an exact replica of the former Inn. By November of 1993 the doors reopened and proudly welcomed guests back with unparalleled hospitality.

There have not really been the same kind of sightings at the Oban Inn, but the staff has reported feeling things that were "not quite right" about the place. One of the theories suggests that the ghosts had moved after the fire to the Oban House, a rental cottage beside the Inn. Visitors staying there have reported jewelery appearing on the bedstand—only to disappear soon after, and then reappear on the day they had planned to check out. Others have seen a male figure lurking at the foot of the bed.

Even if you don't believe in ghosts, you have to wonder how that painting survived the fire. We came across the Oban Inn while making our way from Queen's Park to Fort Mississauga. It's easy to find.

The rental cottage to the right of The Oban Inn.

From the Oban Inn's website: "In 2005, The Oban Inn underwent a significant transformation. Now, with its 26 tranquil, luxurious guest rooms, elegant dining surrounded by delightful ponds and lush English gardens, and the creation of the beautiful new OSpa, the Inn has become a celebrated wellness retreat. OSpa — a unique facility dedicated to the health, well-being and vitality of our guests...soothing and personalized, the philosophy and décor are in harmony with each other, forming a peaceful mood of Sun, Moon, Earth and Water. Our state-of-the-art exercise room has a view of our lush, mature gardens, outdoor hot spring/spa and infinity lap pool."

Pillar and Post

48 John Street
Niagara-on-the-Lake
www.vintage-hotels.com/niagara-on-the-lake/hotels.php

T he original canning factory was built in the late 1890s. You can still see some of the original building in the clean lines of the brick walls and in the post-and-beam construction. Today, the Pillar and Post is a five-star country inn.

"The hotel has a relaxed elegance, sunshine streaming in through skylights, and beautiful terra cotta tile floors. With our attentive service and commitment to the comfort of our guests, it's an ideal location for a family vacation or business meeting. The Pillar and Post's 100 Fountain Spa is an escape to relaxation and tranquility. The recent extensive renovation into a 13,000 square foot spa has resulted in not only a stunning interior, but a wider offering of services, making it top of its class in Ontario. The heated saltwater pools and hot springs, plus a fitness centre, are yours to enjoy during your stay." (www.vintage-hotels.com/ niagara-on-the-lake/hotels/pillar-and-post.php)

The Pillar and Post is a wonderful place to stay, posh and beautiful, a traveler's dream. Unless of course, you happen to get either room 118 or 222. You could be in for a nightmare. At least, that is what people keep reporting despite the efforts of a few people to deny the stories and sweep them under the carpet. Not every establishment wants you to know you might have company as you look forward to a restful sleep at night.

I have been sitting here reading many written accounts from both *Niagara's Ghosts 2* and from the Ontario Ghosts and Hauntings website (www.torontoghosts.org/niagara/pillarpost.htm) and I'm already hoping I get to stay in one of these rooms myself one day. Not only for the wonderful rooms and services, but to meet these ghosts myself.

There are reports of a woman in 1920s style clothing that walks down the stairs into the café area, but she disappears before reaching the main floor. Teacups and saucers mysteriously find their way onto the tables in the café. That sounds harmless enough and if you're lucky, you might catch a glimpse of her.

In room 118, two English women's voices have been heard. So far, they seem to be friendly and quite lively. On the other hand, room 222 is said to have another female presence that slams doors and steals jewelery. She also messes around with the various electronic equipment, turning them on and off.

A woman who had worked on the cleaning staff at the Pillar and Post had contacted Kyle Upton, a ghost tour guide, to tell him about her experience in room 118. She found the clock radio turned on when she entered the room. The music playing sounded like Victorian Christmas songs with a harpsichord and similar old-sounding instruments. She let the music play while she finished her work in the room and enjoyed the music until she was done and went to leave the room. When she turned off the radio, the music continued to play. Assuming there was something wrong with the buttons or the radio itself, she reached behind the side table and unplugged the radio completely. The music continued to play. Flipping the radio over she opened up the latch underneath where the batteries were usually kept, only to find that it was empty.

Holding the radio with no batteries in one hand and the plug in the other, she decided to show her manager that the radio was still playing since she didn't know what else to do. When she put the radio on his desk and it continued to play, he explained the problem. The manager followed her back to room 118 with the clock-radio, and placed it back in the correct spot and plugged it back in. Standing at the door, he spoke to the room and said, "Okay ladies, you can listen to your music, but I've got guests coming in 45 minutes, so you need to shut it off by then," and he closed the door behind him. When she checked back before the guests checked in, the room was silent.

Both aforementioned sources also include a detailed report from a visitor from the United States. He had promised to take his girlfriend to the Pillar and Post for the American Labour Day on September 2, 2001. With no previous knowledge of the Pillar and Post, he simply booked a room, and agreeing with the suggestion of the staff member he had spoken to on the phone, he upgraded to a room with a fireplace.

When he and his girlfriend showed up before they were expected, they were told that an early check-in would not be a problem since they did not specify a room in particular other than one that had a fireplace. The computer had them booked specifically for room 118 and it was locked onto that booking somehow, leaving them unable to make a room change in order to check-in earlier. The couple left to have a late lunch at the Kiely House and did some window shopping.

When they returned and checked into the room, they enjoyed the amenities. Turning the fireplace on and grabbing a couple of chocolate bars from the honour bar, they decided to go for a swim and to relax in the hot tub. He asked his girlfriend to turn the fireplace off. She did. When they returned an hour later the fireplace was on. He gave her a little bit of a hard time about it, but she was sure she did indeed turn the fireplace off when they left to go swimming. Thinking nothing of it, they dressed to go out on the town for the night.

An advertisement she found brought them to the Lantern-lit Ghost Tour of Fort George. Kyle Upton's tour of Fort George started in a wooded area and he spoke about the various haunted Inns and hotels including the Oban Inn, the Kiely House, and the Pillar and Post. When they told him that they were indeed staying at the Pillar and Post, he continued to describe the various happenings in rooms 222 and 118.

His girlfriend gasped and buried her head in her boyfriend's chest. They tried to laugh it off, but he could not help but figure out the odds of them staying in one of the only two rooms that were said to be haunted. He didn't believe in ghosts and had worked as a police officer for fifteen years, and she had her Masters Degree in Psychology and Special Education. Both being smart people, he knew he and his girlfriend would not be easily fooled.

As a part of the tour, Kyle led the group into an underground tunnel. He took this chance to scare his girlfriend just a little bit and hung back from the rest of the group in the tour while they were still in the tunnel. When she looked behind to see if anyone was left behind her, she screamed in sheer terror. Still holding his hand she ran towards the front of the group, barging past another couple directly in front of them. He accidentally stepped on the man's foot and was barely able to recognize a blond woman from the room they had just left at the opposite end of the tunnel.

When they emerged and rejoined the rest of the group she was trying to laugh, but he could tell that she was actually quite shaken up. He tried to get her to tell him what happened and she pointed to the blond woman and the man whose foot he'd stepped on and accused them of rushing up from behind them and passing them in the tunnel. Hearing and seeing this, the other couple was not very amused with what she had to say. They were ahead of them the entire time. He decided to stop teasing her about the ghost stories for the rest of the tour.

Before they left, they stopped to ask Kyle once again about the Pillar and Post room where they were about to return for the night. He told them that people had not seen the ghosts, but strange things such as the fireplace being turned on and the music playing was more common. He told Kyle about how the computer had locked them into the room, not allowing them to change rooms when they went to check-in. His girlfriend had decided that if the fireplace was back on when they returned she would not be able to stay the night.

When they got back to the hotel, she listened at the door instead of going right in and she turned white. Telling him to listen as well, he refused and just walked right into the room without any further hesitation.

The radio was on. She let out another horrified scream and disturbed several of the other patrons who opened their doors to find out what was happening. He calmed her down again, and figured the snooze was accidentally on, or the previous person staying in the room had set the alarm to go off at an odd time, or they had left the radio on before and didn't realize. The radio switch was off, there was no alarm set at all, and there was no snooze button that was hit that turned on the radio. The clock was set to the right time, so there were no power glitches that might have turned the clock off and back on again.

He decided to ignore it and talked her into ordering room service. When he told the waiter who brought their food what had happened so that they might check into the matter, the waiter turned pale and told him that the staff were not supposed to talk to the guests about such things and quickly made his way back down the hallway. Amused, he calmed his girlfriend down again and finished their food. She wanted to leave a night light on, but he argued against it and it took her a long time before she was able to fall asleep.

Before five in the morning, he was awakened by the sensation of someone tugging at his blankets. He felt strangely disoriented, and he could not see anyone at the foot of his bed. He checked to see if his girlfriend was trying to get him back by yanking on the blankets herself. He could hear and see that she was sleeping soundly, and had not been sitting up. He went back to sleep, trying to ignore what could have been a dream. Once again, he felt three or four hard tugs on the blankets from the foot of the bed once again. It was not funny to him anymore.

He turned on the lights and asked his girlfriend if she was awake. He looked around the room, but found nobody in there with them. Not wanting to scare her in the middle of the night, he told her it was nothing. He left a light on for the rest of the evening and did not tell her about the blankets being pulled on his side. He didn't sleep after it happened.

He later reflected on the story that he'd heard about the two older women and concluded that the older women would want the heat of the blanket on such a chilly night, and the fire on that afternoon to keep them warm. Perhaps they were also lonely and wanted to listen to the radio? He still maintains that he does not believe in ghosts and is not afraid of them in the light of day, "but I WON'T be staying in room 118 anytime soon."

Another part of the haunting that the Ontario Ghosts and Hauntings website talks about takes place in the dining area. There are large wooden pillars throughout the dining area and when staff and patrons walk around these pillars they experience the sensation of "walking through" somebody who disappears on the other side. This same ghost has been seen walking right through the pillars as well. The people who do not know about the haunting have stumbled across (or into) this apparition and have gotten quite the scare. In some cases the staff cannot handle the sightings and have quit their job.

Someone who had lived in Niagara-on-the-Lake for twenty-five years wrote in to the website to debunk the stories about the Pillar and Post. He had even worked at the Pillar and Post himself for eight years. He said that he never saw or heard anything like what was reported. He also mentioned having known people who worked there since the early 1970s who also had never heard such a thing. Giving kudos to the hotel itself, he also wrote about his frustration with the claims of haunting for so many places in the Niagara region out of attempts just to boost business. He also made a joke that made me laugh about the only undead in the place would be some bellhops roaming aimlessly.

Both his message and the message from the American boyfriend with his scared girlfriend were sent on the exact same day—October 22, 2001. The American read his response and replied in turn. He assured everyone that the staff was certainly not boasting about their unseen visitors. Quite the opposite, they were trying to keep it quiet and the staff was told not to talk about it at all. He also made clear that what he saw was probably not a ghost, but a curious string of coincidences. The experience opened his mind, however, and he is not comfortable telling everyone he knows about it. He added, "Believe me, in the light of day I would never tell my co-workers about this experience, but in the dark of night with something tugging on your blankets, see if you can sleep."

It wasn't until a few years later that some of the staff at the Pillar and Post spoke up again to tell more about the things that they saw and heard. In 2005 someone who had worked for the Vintage Inns and specifically at the Pillar and Post had heard many credible stories.

One of the girls bussing the tables in the dining room had forgotten her name tag. She took an extra one from the hostess stand and wore that for the night.

Throughout the evening, she felt like someone had tugged on her ponytail. Thinking nothing of it, she continued to work as usual. It wasn't until she also felt someone pulling on her shirt as she climbed the stairs. When she went to serve a drink from her tray to a customer, the glass just tipped itself over. The people at her table commented on how strange it was for a glass to knock over the way it did since she was standing perfectly still. She said it felt like someone had hit the tray in her hand. At the end of the night when everyone was finishing up and cleaning the dining room, she was telling a server about the events she'd experienced. The server recognized the nametag as having belonged to someone who used to work there years before. The original waitress also felt her hair and shirt being pulled on every shift she'd worked. When she could not deal with it anymore, she quit. It was the same nametag that read "Diana" and the tag was promptly thrown into the garbage.

The same person had a report about Colonel John Butler.

John Butler was born in New London, Connecticut in 1728. His father was an officer in the British Army that had come to North America to participate in the expedition of Quebec in 1711. John was about fourteen during the years of the French and Indian wars when he followed his older brothers into the British Indian Department of Sir William Johnson. One of his places of action was in the Niagara region. During the peace following the conquest of Canada, John inherited the land that his father left behind.

"At the outbreak of the Revolution, he moved to Montreal with the Indian Department and was dispatched to Niagara in November of 1775 to manage the department there. His eldest son, Walter, accompanied him, but his wife and the remaining children were held prisoners by the rebels. John Butler led a strong detachment of Indians from Niagara at the Battle of Oriskany in August of 1777. His success during the battle led to the authorization to raise a Corps of Rangers to serve with the Indians on the frontiers. The Corps informally came to be known as Butler's Rangers. At the end of the Revolution, Butler once again turned to farming, and became the 'de facto' leader of the settlement in the Niagara Peninsula. He served as Deputy Superintendent of the Indian Department at Niagara, a Justice of the Peace, a member of the Land Board of Niagara, Lieutenant of the County of Lincoln, Commanding Officer of the Nassau and Lincoln militia, leader of the Church of England in the community, and a prominent member of the Masonic Order. Butler died at Niagara on 12 May 1796, after a long illness." (http://www. iaw.on.ca/~awoolley/brang/brbutler.html)

There is a portrait of John Butler hanging on the wall beside one of the doorways. At the end of the night the bartenders would close the door leading to the dining room. While counting the till, she heard something coming from the doorway and upon inspection, the door was open. Nobody was there. After closing the door again, she tripped in the same spot where she often snagged their foot. There are two armchairs facing the painting — it was said that it was the Colonel's favourite portrait of himself and he often sat in the chair to admire it — it was in front of the armchair that she tripped, yet again. Is the Colonel still sitting there?

Those were her personal stories. This staff member also backed up the American boyfriend's stories about the radio in room 118 as she had heard the radio go on and off herself. She also stated that she was not superstitious.

Within the week of that posting, someone else wrote in to state that even though they worked at the Pillar and Post, and were believers in ghosts, they never saw anything during the time they were employed at the Inn.

Is it haunted? Yes. No. Yes. No. I'm starting to feel like I'm riding a ghostly see-saw. The people who saw and heard strange things are just as adamant as the people who have never experienced anything out of the ordinary. A manager for the Vintage Hotels who has only spent a short time at the Pillar and Post believes the stories of the traveling Americans. Being a believer himself, he has not yet seen or heard anything, but promises to report back as soon as he does.

I encourage you to go and visit the Pillar and Post yourselves, treat yourself to the wonderful services, and meet the great hotel staff. See if you end up walking into someone around a pillar. Check out Colonel John Butler's favourite portrait and have a seat in the chair to admire it for a while. If you dare, ask to stay in room 118 or 222. If you do and you experience anything, I'd love to hear your stories. Even if you don't believe what you see or hear, maybe someone else will.

Queen's Royal Park

On the Niagara River
at King Street

The Gazebo at Queen's Royal Park.

The 1983 movie, "The Dead Zone" by David Cronenburg, was filmed at many locations at Niagara-on-the-Lake. The Gazebo in Queen's Royal Park was built for that movie and has since become the spot of many tourist and wedding pictures. As a matter of fact, I've been in a wedding party and had pictures taken in and around the Gazebo. While on the Walking Ghost Tour by Haunted Hamilton, we were told that the tour guide often had tourists who had pictures taken that showed additional men lining up to get in the picture. (There were no unexpected guests in the wedding photos I was in years ago.)

If you know where Fort Mississauga is, you can see that the rocky shore was not a place where anybody could land and move forward in battle, but the beach area at Queen's Royal Park made a better opportunity for soldiers to come to shore. It is about a ten minute leisurely walk from the Park to Fort Mississauga. Fort Niagara is in plain sight and it would have been a short trip across the lake to attack. It is unknown how many soldiers from each side might have died down on that beach.

There is also a "Lady in White" that has been seen walking along the beach. There have been a few people who have reported seeing her in a couple of their pictures as well. Others have seen her walking along the beach as clearly as

Above: The Haunted Hamilton guide on our winter Walking Ghost Tour.
Opposite: The beach by the Gazebo at Queen's Royal Park.

if she was a real person taking a stroll at night, before disappearing completely.

I took a few pictures in the dark…wondering if anyone would show up. It's fun to get carried away a little bit. I didn't see anything out of the ordinary in any of my pitch black pictures. I wonder if the 'lady' was waiting for a soldier to come back to her, or if there is another circumstance that leads her to continually walk the beach after death.

Prince of Wales

6 Picton Street
Niagara-on-the-Lake
www.vintage-hotels.com/niagara-on-the-lake/hotels/
prince-of-wales.php

The Prince of Wales Hotel at night in Niagara-on-the-Lake.

One of Niagara's most luxurious hotels is the Prince of Wales.

"Located in the heart of historic Niagara-on-the-Lake, the Prince of Wales is an oasis of Victorian elegance filled with 21st century comforts. The hotel was named in honour of a royal visit in 1901, when the future George V stayed here. Today, every guest experiences the sophistication and refinement of that bygone age." (http://www.vintage-hotels.com/niagara-on-the-lake/hotels/prince-of-wales.php)

The owners and staff at the Prince of Wales might tell you that there used to be paranormal activity, but that you won't find it there anymore. Unfortunately, there are still certain rooms where patrons have checked out in the middle of the night due to some disturbances as late as the year 2002.

There just might be an older woman who resides in what used to be the Hotel Library who likes to follow the staff, move objects, and close or knock on doors in the hallway. Some believe that this is the spirit of Molly McGuire who died in 1813 when an American soldier stabbed her in the back. ("Molly McGuire" is also the name of a band, a singer, a pub, and a secret Irish terrorist association that formed in 1843 where members disguised themselves as women — a fascinating story unto itself.)

Sobbing Sophia

Brockamour Manor
433 King Street, Niagara-on-the-Lake
www.brockamour.com

In 1809, when Captain Powell built his home for his wife and family in Newark (now Niagara-on-the-Lake), his sister-in-law Sophia, joined them. (Their father, Aeneas Shaw, was a frequent visitor.) As destiny would have it, this move led to Sophia meeting Isaac Brock, a stunning young man who was made a Brigadier-General in 1808, with whom she completely fell in love. Brock traveled from one end of the Province of Upper Canada to the other as tensions grew between Britain and the United States. His travels often brought him to the home of Captain Powell to speak with Aeneas Shaw about war, and about his love of Shaw's daughter, Sophia.

They were never able to afford a wedding or a proper home, but very few people ever knew about Brock's difficulties. There were certain secrets he told only to Sophia, and only the two of them knew about their private engagement. On the morning of October 13, 1812, Brock heard cannons being fired and he made only one stop before racing into battle on horseback. Sophia made him a cup of coffee to help keep him warm and they said a very quick goodbye. It was the last time she saw him alive before he was shot by an American marksman.

Sophia and her sister, Isabella (who was also widowed), lived in the house that came to be known as Brockamour, or "love of Brock," and Sophia Shaw's sobbing can still be heard in the building.

Listen carefully for the cries that will forever go out to her love, Isaac Brock.

The Screaming Tunnel

The Screaming Tunnel.

A little harder to find, you'd have to make sure you don't miss the Glendale exit off of the QEW. Make a left on Taylor Road (South Service Road), and another left onto Warner and it's just past the Garner intersection. You found it? Good. Of course if you just open your window, you could follow your nose. It stinks of (at least) sulphur.

The tunnel was originally built by the Grand Trunk Railway (GTR) Company, North America's first international railroad, just before the outbreak of World War I in their grand scheme to have a railway that ran the same grounds as the Welland Canal. By 1914 the project was abandoned due to financial hardships. The railway was a financial disaster and was largely responsible for the bankruptcy of the GTR in 1919. Sadly, tunnels were built and then totally given up with the outbreak of the war. The "Screaming Tunnel" is one of a few of these railway tunnels that lead to nowhere, made for a railroad line that never existed.

It was meant to be a forgotten tunnel, but it became the site of a wonderful ghost story. Many versions of the story have been passed down from one generation to the next. I personally enjoy finding obscure locations for ghost tales, and I had already visited the location years ago with G and some friends. It was a cold autumn day, and we stayed in the tunnel for as long as we could stand the wind. The ground was wet from the November rains, and the stone walls offered little protection. Not a pleasant place to hang out for very long, we tried to listen for any faint sounds. I tried flipping my lighter on to see if it would be blown out, as I had heard that would happen at the time.

Unfortunately, I didn't know enough about the various versions of the stories about the tunnel back then.

Soon after the Screaming Tunnel was created and left unused, there was a massive fire in a farmhouse just on the south side of the tunnel. A young girl came running out of the burning building covered in flames, screaming into the night. In an attempt to extinguish the flames in the wet ground of the tunnel, she collapsed to the floor and died alone.

Perhaps that wasn't all there was to the story? Maybe she was set on fire by her abusive father when he found out that his wife had won custody of the children during a terrible divorce battle? Or, this young girl was raped in the tunnel and set ablaze to hide the evidence? Or, was there simply a party in that house and an accident with a candle caused the fire? Other versions include curses, evil demons, various forms of murder, on Halloween, at midnight, during the middle of the day... Whatever is in there, whoever was in there, is said to react to open flames. This is why I had tried to use my lighter when I was in the tunnel the first time years ago. However, another version of the story says that you have to use a wooden match while standing in the middle of the tunnel specifically. If you do go in there and light a match, you're supposed to hear a horrible, shrilling scream, followed by your match being blown out.

A local favourite spot for partying, you will find broken glass, graffiti, and other evidence of young people spending a Saturday night trying to scare each other. I wonder how many "eye witnesses" came from those nights of frivolity and allowing themselves to be vulnerable to the various stories. At what point does it make the tale an urban myth?

What if that tunnel, which is very windy, is just a windy tunnel? That would certainly make a match blow out, or even a lighter. Could the wind also catch the top of the tunnel at just the right speed and make a high pitched sound? I don't know. My lighter didn't go out, and none of us heard anything during the time we could stand being in the dank passageway. Maybe we should try it at midnight instead of the middle of the day? Or on Halloween? Maybe you should try it.

G and I went back down to visit the tunnel recently on a summer Saturday afternoon. A train passed over the tunnel and I was able to catch a short video and pictures while I was there. As we expected, there was graffiti all around the entrance off the street, and broken bottles. I'd almost forgotten how distinct the sulphur smell was until we got within fifty feet. A small creek drained through the middle of the pathway with some stones on the side to walk on towards the other end. Some of the stones along the top arch were wet or dripping on us. About half way through, we found matches on the ground. They looked new, and we assumed they were used just the night before as they hadn't even been walked on or weathered yet. All together there must have been about thirty long, wooden fireplace matches strewn all over the ground. Somebody had been there the night before looking for this ghost and believed that they would hear the

Wet walls and small stream on the ground inside the Screaming Tunnel.

Some of the long, fireplace matches.

scream and have their matches extinguished. We wondered if they actually heard anything. I don't doubt the matches were blown out on them, it's quite a windy tunnel and none of the matches looked like they had burnt down for any length of time. Do you think they heard the screams?

If that's not spooky enough, I've got another little detail for you. The Screaming Tunnel was also used for a scene in David Cronenburg's 1983 movie, "The Dead Zone" with Christopher Walken. What would be scarier, going down there yourself... or asking Christopher Walken if he went in there?

Queen Victoria Park Restaurant (Refectory)

www.cliftonhill.com/niagara_falls_restaurants/victoria_park/

The Queen Victoria Park Restaurant is known for its family dining, outdoor terrace, relaxing Beer Garden, and live entertainment. It is located between the Table Rock House and the American Falls on the Niagara Parkway.

The building originally built in 1860 was Thomas Barnett's Museum. Construction began in April 1859. Barnett, seeking the best possible building for his collection, sent to England for an "original" museum plan. The final product was very ornate and elaborate, much like other museums built in the nineteenth century. Outside, the three-story museum was decorated with a colonnade facade and a stained glass window above the entrance. The museum also had large greenhouses where there were beautiful gardens; a huge pond with waterfowl, zoological enclosures that contained buffalo, wolves, deer and birds; extensive picnic grounds, and huge Native American wigwams. The museum complex was located on what was known as "The Front," a highly commercialized plot of land bordering the Falls. In 1887, the Niagara Parks Commission was formed to convert "The Front" to the present Q.V.P. — Queen Victoria Park. The museum was forced to relocate.

By 1889, the Dufferin Café moved in and lasted until 1902. The building was then demolished and a new one was built in 1904 modeled after a Swiss chalet (not the well known chain of restaurants, an actual Swiss chalet). The new Refectory Restaurant moved in. In 1939, during World War II, the Refectory Restaurant was the closest point where tourists could view the Falls when military forces guarded all hydro electric power plants by laying barbed wire barriers. Niagara Parks administrative staff moved to the Refectory and established their offices in the Commissioner's Quarters in 1907. The administrative staff moved out in 1926.

It is in the Commissioner's Quarters where the ghosts have been seen many times over the last twenty-five years. There is a man dressed in a tuxedo who has been seen walking around. You might also catch a glimpse of the "Pink Lady," dressed in formal attire from the late nineteenth century. There have also been some strange sounds coming from the Commissioner's Quarters.

Lewiston McDonald'sÆ

The Frontier House
Center Street
Lewiston, New York

It is said that William Morgan died on September 13, 1826 long before it was turned into a McDonald's. The McDonald's was located in Lewiston's Frontier House, one of the region's oldest buildings (originally the westernmost stop of the Barton Stage Line and later a Masonic Temple), where the Masons used to hold meetings. Previous ghost hunters have claimed that Morgan got into some trouble with the Masons and threatened to publish the secrets of the Masonic order. How he died is still a mystery. In the 1970s a manager said he saw a ghost, and he'd heard strange things and that doors would open and close. Cleaning staff reported seeing a white image of an old man who appeared in the pantry. A maintenance man quit after another sighting. If you ate downstairs, you might have felt a cold breeze or heard a man crying out for help.

However, it has been abandoned since 2004 and there has been some talk about starting a culinary school on the first floor.

Niagara Falls Clet Hall

Clet Hall at the Niagara University has burned down multiple times, resulting in numerous deaths. One of the ghosts is of a student who died in a fire. Many students have claimed to see his ghost inside their dorm rooms and in the adjacent theatre.

Tonawanda Elmlawn Church/Cemetery

A young woman married the love of her life in Elmlawn Church. Excited after the ceremony, the two made their way out and across the street to the romantic carriage that was ready to whisk them away. She was run over by a carriage coming up the road, and was killed instantly.

Some people say that you can still see her crossing the road after dark. Others say that you can see orbs of light, or a number of unidentified lights between the hours of midnight and three in the morning.

The Apothecary

5 Queen Street
Niagara-on-the-Lake
www.niagaraapothecary.ca/

The Apothecary, closed today.

The Niagara Apothecary was in full operation for one hundred years under six different owners until it closed in 1964. Early in the nineteenth century, pharmaceutical and other medicinal supplies were not available locally and shipments had to be delivered from England or Europe. Due to the long wait, the orders had to be large enough to ensure there were enough supplies to last them until the next shipment would arrive. Codeine became available in gel capsules, and ether and chloroform were used for surgery by the 1840s. Suddenly, they had remedies for everything and they claimed to heal the most incredible and bizarre illnesses. The Ontario Heritage Foundation reopened the building as a museum in 1971. The Apothecary website has some very interesting stories about when certain drugs such as Aspirin were available, and what it was like during the time of each of the six owners. Every time we have gone to visit the Apothecary, it has been closed.

There have been reports that footsteps can be heard running up and down the back staircase that has stayed generally enclosed. To try to find out what was going on, newspapers were laid carefully all over the steps and even though nobody was seen coming or going, the newspapers were all disturbed. Others say that they can smell fresh flowers, or even stranger, Belladonna (also known as "Deadly Nightshade," a seeming cure-all for many illnesses but a poison in large quantities) even though it hasn't been kept on the premises

The Apothecary:
A view through the window at all of the small bottles and medical items on display.

for decades. Some people have also noticed various cold spots throughout the building. I have yet to find a story that explains who this could be walking up and down the back stairs, but one day soon, I'd like to go back and keep my ears and nose on alert for anything strange. Not that I'd know what Belladonna smells like.

Fort Mississauga

*FORE! The Fort is located on the grounds
of the Niagara-on-the-Lake Golf Club*

The entrance to Fort Mississauga, which is located in the middle of a
Golf Course.

Originally back in the fifteenth century, the area was a Neutral First Nation fishing settlement. By the seventeenth century the area was under control of the Seneca Nation, and then by the Mississauga Nation at the beginning of the eighteenth century. In 1804, a lighthouse was erected at the site, which had become known as Mississauga Point, the first lighthouse on the Great Lakes.

Parts of the lighthouse were used to build the Fort.

When Fort George was destroyed During the War of 1812 by American troops, Fort Mississauga was strategically built to help British and Canadian forces defend Niagara against the American army. The lighthouse was dismantled and some of the stone was incorporated along with the rubble found in the town of Newark after the Americans burnt down the entire town. The brick and stone foundation was used to create an all brick central tower that was completed after the war was over in 1814 and served as an emergency field reinforcement.

Fort Mississauga is the only example of a star shaped earthwork in Canada. (Earthworks could have high stone or brick, or huge walls of dirt such as Fort Mississauga. Some earthworks are surrounded by deep moats, or they could be low mounds of dirt that were quickly shovelled up when under fire.) They mark the spot on the battlefield where the soldiers stood and defined the lines of battle, and they show the strategic importance of the ground

Earthworks surrounded by a small moat that helped guard their lines around Fort Mississauga.

itself. Fort Mississauga was one part of a defense system including Fort George, Butler's Barracks, and Fort Erie.

The British were stationed there until 1855, and in the 1870s the Fort was used as a summer training camp throughout both World Wars and the Korean War.

"Mr. Hunter and J. Geale Dickson laid out the first golf course in Niagara, the Fort George course, in 1877. The next year they made a course on the Fort Mississauga common." (*Looking Back: Niagara-on-the-Lake Ontario*, 96)

In the *Lake Ontario Waterfront Network News*, #3/01, July 3, 2001 it is reported that the Friends of Fort George had "completed a new stretch of trail along the Niagara-on-the-Lake (NOTL) waterfront. The trail begins at Front and Simcoe streets, crosses the NOTL Golf Club and follows the contour of the abandoned Fort Mississauga. Once on the grounds of the Fort, the trail leads people to the dramatic junction of the Niagara River and Lake Ontario."

Even though it is open to the public, Fort Mississauga is not an official tourist destination due to the lack of facilities and services. It is also one of the only Forts in Ontario that has not been restored. There are a couple of tunnels you can follow into the powder magazines in the earthworks, and another that leads to the lake where you can see Fort Niagara.

If you follow the pedestrian trail that begins at the corner of Simcoe and Front streets (just on the other side of Queen's Park), be careful as you walk through the golf course. Parks Canada urges on its website: "For safety reasons the public must remain on the marked trail at all times until inside the fort. The public must allow golfers to complete their shots before proceeding, and look

It was important to be able to see Fort Niagara through the trees and to not be seen as easily by their enemies across the lake.

carefully to ensure that the way is clear. Children should be attended at all times. No bicycles, scooters, roller blades, skateboards, or other vehicles are allowed."

Is there anything else you should be careful of when you go to visit Fort Mississauga? Some people think so. The Ontario Ghosts and Hauntings Research Society (GHRS) heard a story from someone who goes by the name of Ashley, the white witch of Niagara. She told them about an "unfortunate aboriginal whose head was literally shot-off with a cannon strike from Fort Niagara on the American side. This sad man now wanders the fort sans head." What she failed to take into account was that the fort was not completed until the end of the war when the British already had control of the surrounding forts.

Another person from St. Catherine's said that he and his friends saw the ghost of a soldier being whipped on

A view from inside the earthworks, and somewhere along that wall was where Andrew Greenhill saw the apparitions.

the earthworks surrounding the Fort. GHRS tried to get some more details about the apparition of the flogging from this person afterwards, but received no response. Kyle Upton also writes (in *Niagara's Ghosts 2*) that "many claim that the ghost of a soldier that was flogged to death can be seen walking the ruins of the old Fort." He also mentions that there is a special spot on the golf course, if you can find it, where you can hear the sounds of the battle of Fort George from 1813. Apparently some people have found the spot and did indeed hear the sounds of invisible armies at battle. I would love to know where this spot is located.

The following passage is an account from a soldier posted at Fort Mississauga in the Canadian Military History (*Autumn 2003*, 37-54). Andrew Greenhill writes about what he saw on the morning of June 11, 1871:

> "One of the rooms in the central tower was occupied by the guard. The first two hours off Jim and I spread our blankets on the hard oak floor and slept as sound as a top the whole time. We had to turn out at 2 a.m. Jim was put on the gate and I on the ramparts. It was pitch dark and the time dragged wearily along. The only sound that broke the deathlike stillness was the waves washing against the lake front of the fort. The only thing we saw in that long two hours were a dog & a tall figure in a black robe. It glided along the top of the wall swiftly & was seen by Jim as well as myself. My knees shook under me. I fixed my bayonet, gave chase & challenged but it glided out of sight & left me more frightened than ever. We said nothing to the guard about it after being afraid of the ridicule."

My husband and I went to visit Fort Mississauga on a sunny day in April. We were surprised to find how close it was to Queen's Park since you can't even see it from the Gazebo. When we found the beginning of the trail, we saw a sign that explains the need to be careful along the path because of the golfers. I thought we would be walking between holes where the golf carts might be zipping along. You start off walking side by side with the first hole tee-off, and soon after that, you end up walking right in front of a tee-off for another hole. Two golfers had to wait for us to pass. You are really in the line of fire walking this path, and thankfully, it's not that far to go as you can see the Fort right away. There was no way we would have been able to find the haunted spot on the course where we could hear the battle without taking our own lives into our hands.

I was expecting the earthworks to be higher, but when I saw the small moat and tried to imagine what it would take to get through the moat and up the hill, soldiers would have easily seen them coming on the other side. I was reminded of the weapons they had used and how effective the fort really would have been in that kind of bloody combat. Once inside, we felt light years away from a golf course. The stone and brick fort crumbled in spots. The very narrow windows were barred up and the

The entrance to one of the powder magazines.

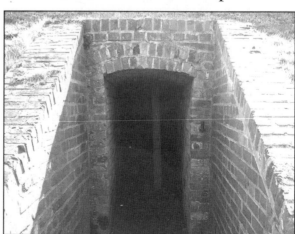

single small entry door was locked up tight. We really wished we could have gone in, but knew that it was a safety hazard. One of the cool and damp tunnels to the powder magazines was full of graffiti, the other was not. We had to crouch slightly to fit inside, and the width only allowed one person at a time inside.

We read several historical plaques around the fort and checked out the tunnel to the lake, which led to a steep, stone walkway. We did not see any ghosts as described in the earlier stories, perhaps because it wasn't midnight. However, we did feel something while we were inside the fort area. Perhaps it was because we knew and respected the events that had happened there so many years ago, and being able to imagine the battles and brutal deaths. Maybe it was because we already knew about the ghost stories.

We felt a strange intensity, a certain pressure around and in the fort that threw us into the Old World on a beautiful summer day.

Some people would argue it was caused by a ghostly presence, or a spiritual impression left behind. From our own experience, I would argue the latter, if anything.

Part of the inside of one the very small powder magazines.

A Peek
into the Life

A Private in the British
regular army during
the War of 1812 would
have been accustomed to:
1. Wearing a leather collar (as
would his American counterpart)
to prevent him from becoming
distracted in battle
by the sight of fallen comrades.
2. Carrying 60 lbs (27 kg) of gear, much of
it in a haversack with a wooden frame that
would cut into his back on long marches.
3. Receiving pay of one shilling
per day (about ten cents
today) before costs were
deducted for food, medicine, etc.
4. Punishment of up to 300 whiplashes
for behaviour contrary to regulations.
5. Drills and more drills, interspersed only
by periods of unmitigated boredom.
6. Cooking and eating his own meals twice a day,
early in the morning and at noon.
7. Consuming rum instead of contaminated water.
The U.S. Army favoured Whiskey.
8. Being drunk much of the time (see #7), resulting in
receiving punishment (i.e. lashes) for misconduct.
(The Niagara Frontier: Its Place in U.S. and Canadian History; 58)

Fort George

Located on the Niagara Parkway
Niagara-on-the-Lake
www.friendsoffortgeorge.ca/
Ghost Tours: www.psican.org/ghrs/ghosttours/

Stepping inside the front doors of Fort George.

If you want to know about the ghosts in Fort George, Kyle Upton is the man to talk to. Not only has he been running ghost tours for over a decade, he has worked in the fort by day, which is also a historical park and tourist attraction. When I got in touch with him in 2006 and told him about what I was working on, he sent me a copy of his book, *Niagara's Ghosts 2*, for reference. It was killing me to wait until May 2007 to go on the ghost tour myself. I'd like to share with you some of the stories that Kyle told us on the tour, some of which are in his book, and I'll also tell you about what some of the people in the group experienced...including me.

First, a brief history. In 1796, the British began work on Fort George and it was completed in 1802, specifically built on the opposite side of the Niagara River from the American Fort Niagara. Boasting six earthen and log fortresses linked by a wooden stakes, it was also surrounded by a dry ditch. Inside they constructed a guardhouse, log blockhouses, a hospital, kitchens, workshops, barracks, officers' quarters, and a stone powder magazine.

At the beginning of the War of 1812 in October, it was the headquarters of Isaac Brock and housed the British Army, Upper Canadian Militia, and the Six Nations Warriors. The Americans attacked and after twelve hours of battle (when a sniper killed Isaac Brock), the American army was defeated. In May of 1813, the fort was attacked again and destroyed by artillery fire and captured by the Americans. The only original building to survive to this day is the Powder Magazine with four-foot-thick walls, and is the oldest military structure in Ontario. They used the fort as a base for invading Upper Canada, but were forced to retreat after the battles of Stoney Creek and Beaver Dams. By the 1820s it was falling into ruins and it was abandoned in favour of Fort Mississauga and Butler's Barracks. The fort was retaken by British forces and partially rebuilt after the war.

The fort that stands today was rebuilt in the 1930s by the Niagara Parks Commission, and is now maintained by Parks Canada.

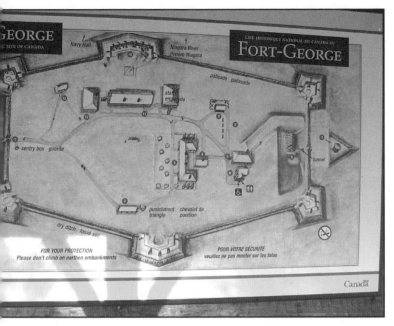

Too large to get the entire fort in one picture without a plane, this is the layout of Fort George that is supplied by Parks Canada.

Brock and his aide-de-camp John MacDonnell were initially buried within the Fort. There were hundreds of soldiers who were buried inside and outside of the fort, often in the very spot where they died, scattered in unmarked graves. Families of soldiers and officers lived inside the fort, raising their families in the blockhouses, and when they managed to survive the winter weather, the battles were still to come. But I'm getting ahead of myself now.

G and I went down to the park early to get some clear pictures while the sun was still out. We walked around the outside of the fort. There were families gathered around having picnics, bicycles were either lined up on the rack or ridden down the path in the park, and having been to Fort Mississauga we were both surprised to see how much larger Fort George really was. We'd stopped to read the signs posted about the history and location of the fort. We looked up to see Fort Niagara just on the other side of the Niagara River and saw that the two were in easy range of each other. Tourist signs showed projectiles of cannonballs and other weapons and trajectories across the water.

As we walked around and took some pictures of the wooden-spiked fences and the steep earthworks, we noticed small holes in the walls and wanted to take a closer look. Despite the signs that request people to "Stay off the earthworks" and "Keep away from the Hills" (for your own safety), G slid down one side and I watched him struggle to climb up to the fence. If the original structure was anything close to the present day and the earthworks were the same, there was little chance of attacking this fort on foot and surviving. Cannons peeked through corners and the watchtower on the far end outside of the fort would see you coming from miles away. I crawled into another dry moat and found some ramps to walk out of

Earthworks and moats around the much larger Fort George.

Cannons peeking through corners.

around the watchtower. (But please, obey the signs and stay back. They are very steep.)

A couple of hours later, we met up with Kyle in the parking lot, along with other people that were planning on joining the Walking Ghost Tour. It is suggested that you dress for the weather and wear comfortable shoes for walking on uneven ground. Once the group was collected and ready, we headed for the front gates. Along the way Kyle told us about the history of Fort George and some stories about the other haunted places such as the Angel Inn and the Pillar and Post.

"Niagara-On-The-Lake is the most haunted city in Canada (per capita) and for every one hundred residents in the city, there is also a resident ghost."

Over the years, they figured about sixty percent of the tours have resulted in sightings or strange experiences by the guests, and there was a good chance that someone would see or feel something that night. (But try not to be disappointed if you don't.) He asked that instead of freaking out during the tour, could we please wait until the end to share any stories of occurrences we might have experienced along the way. He stood with the lantern in his hand and recounted the war stories, the bloody battles, and despite how calm the city is now, the past was full of terror and death.

Once inside the gates, we could see from left to right the Blockhouses (1 &2), the Officers' Quarters, and there were cannons in front of the Guardhouse where soldiers would check in and state their business. It was too dark to see anything beyond that despite the perfectly clear and starry night, so we made sure we stayed on the trail until we stopped in front of Blockhouse 1.

Kyle Upton guiding the Walking Ghost Tour of Fort George.

The Blockhouses were the army's warehouse structures that accommodated other ranks of soldiers (below officers) and their families as well as supplies. Generally, the first floor was built for the supplies with high ceilings and the upper floor for people with lower ceilings to keep in heat. The current buildings are larger than the former structures, but they are mostly on the original foundations. For every fifty soldiers living in the Blockhouses you might have found six wives and up to twelve children at any given time, supported by the military. Today, Blockhouse 1 houses a museum display of the Fort and tales of the bloody past. The lights in this building are left on at night, and if you're not paying close attention, some of the articles in the museum, or the support beam in the middle of the floor could really give you a good startle as you walk by because something appears to be moving inside. If you're already aware of this, or aren't tricked by little perspective and light changes, that doesn't mean you're safe from a ghostly scare.

Blockhouse 1

People have started to witness something else in Blockhouse 1 while on the tours as early back as 1994. A shadowy figure appeared to be looking out of the ground floor window, watching them as they walked along the path. As the years went by and the tours continued, more and more tourists saw this strange shadow peering out at them. Eventually, the staff at Fort George also saw this same apparition. Kyle had mentioned a few times that a school of psychics had taken the tour and they noticed that there was a very angry man who paced back and forth in that window. On another tour that consisted of 18-24 year olds, they also saw this pacing figure and went from too cool to be scared to downright panicked. The ghost has been nicknamed The Watcher.

Kyle wasn't convinced. He knows that the lights in the fort can play tricks on your eyes and the power of suggestion is very strong. Something that happened in 1996 brought an end to his skepticism. After the tours, he has to go back into the fort in the darkness to lock up, and during those times, the fort changes from a tourist area to a quiet cemetery atmosphere. On a night that made him feel uncomfortable anyway, Kyle looked up into the lit window of Blockhouse 1 and saw that the light was blocked by a shadow that filled the opening. He had seen ghosts before around the fort and very few times has it affected him emotionally. He describes in his book:

> "I was filled with such a gut level feeling of terror that I contemplated climbing over the 10 foot high wooden palisades to escape from the fort, rather than risk walking past that building to the front gate. In all my life, only nightmares have imparted the same incredible sense of fear." (*Niagara's Ghosts 2*, 43)

Kyle goes on to say that after spending some time in the well-lit staff building, he ventured back out and saw nothing. The Watcher has not bothered him since, but he tries not to look in that window after sunset.

There have been several reports about the appearance of The Watcher. Most of them have claimed to see a caucasian male with dark features silhouetted in the window. Someone else said they saw him screaming with his face covered with blood. Another saw him wearing a red cape. Psychics have not been able to add many more details about him other than one who felt as if he had been murdered in that building. (And another ghost that was the murderer.) Are the two souls bound together forever, replaying those last moments?

Kyle didn't mention it during the tour we went on, but there is a mention of a creature in his book. A story submitted by a woman named Megan starts with the Fort staff keeping watch as the tours ran smoothly back in 2002. Three of them were standing by the Officers' Quarters as Kyle told the group about a mirror. One by one they all saw a figure leaning against Blockhouse 1, and assumed someone new tried to sneak into the fort. As the tour headed back towards the direction of Blockhouse 2, all three staff members confirmed that they saw the figure leaning on the corner of the next building over. When the lantern-led group got closer, the figure took off at an inhuman speed to the back of the fort. Two of the staff decided to chase it and by the time they got to the area they were stopped by the third staff member just long enough for them to lose sight of the creature. They tried to describe what they saw to Kyle. "They wouldn't call it a run, and wouldn't call it a scurry, but the figure definitely used both its arms and legs to move. All three are convinced that no living thing could move that fast." (*Niagara's Ghosts 2*, 48)

We moved on to the next building. Even though I'd worn a jacket, I was starting to feel the spring air giving me a bit of a chill. Luckily, we were led inside Blockhouse 2 and into a heated room where there was a long set of wooden tables and benches where we could sit by candlelight. Even though we were specifically asked not to take flash pictures, I was really tempted to take my camera out and try and catch the image...but I refrained and sat down like a good girl.

Behind us was a line-up of army style bunk beds that are still being used by military camps and there were name tags at the foot of each bed. I reluctantly set my bag with my camera, wallet, phone and notepad on the floor behind me. At the leftmost end of the tables was a wooden staircase that went up to the second level. It was roped off. Beyond that looked like some storage, but it was hard to tell. To the right of the tables was another

Blockhouse 2.

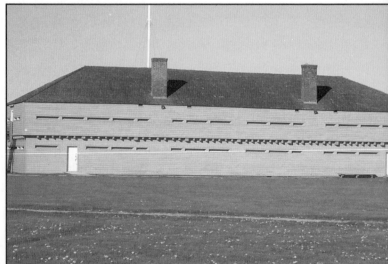

door leading out of the building, closer to Blockhouse 1, and another stairwell leading up to the Barracks. There were shelves all around the room, and in the middle was an iron woodstove. As Kyle told us that the lower floor was originally intended for storage and what it was like to live there year round, my cell phone started beeping.

I felt like a jerk. I should have known to turn it off before the tour even started, and I really regretted having left it on. Not only because it was rude, but because it sucked me out of the past and out of the mood very quickly. Knowing it would keep beeping louder and louder until I turned it off, I grabbed my bag up from the floor, found the blue flickering light, and I saw a message waiting for me before I quickly shut it off.

Blockhouse 2 is the largest of the buildings in the fort, and it is the most haunted. It was also the most visible building from the enemy lines on the American side. The enemies could actually see their cannons ripping the shingles off of the Blockhouse roof as they hit their target early in the morning while everyone was still asleep. Not only the soldiers, but their entire families were in the bunks and died violently before they even knew what happened. One of the images that will be with me for a long time is that of Kyle pointing to the ceiling, showing the path of the ghost they called "Irving."

One night, staff members John and Rick were getting ready to close up for the night after a long day. Before the 1990s there were displays for tourists to see upstairs. When Rick and John started to lock up, they heard footsteps around the upper floor. Not doubting for a second that it was a tourist left behind and not wanting to lock them in the fort for the night, John went up to escort whoever it was out. When he got to the top of the stairs, he saw a man walking from one side of the building to the other. He called out to the man to let him know that they were locking up and that he would have to leave. The man ignored John completely. John tried to make himself heard and spoke louder, again informing the guest that it was closing time, and could he please come down the stairs with him and he'd show him the way out. Again, he was ignored and the man continued to walk across the room. He might have been hard of hearing, or didn't speak English. John decided to walk over to the man while still calling out to him, meaning to reach out and tap him on the shoulder to get his attention. Listening from downstairs, Rick came up to see what the matter was and to help John escort the lost person out of the building. When Rick asked him what was taking so long and reminded him that it was time to go home, John turned to answer him and explained that the gentleman in the room was ignoring him and would not leave.

When John turned back to address the man again, he was gone. John was in an empty room. Was it possible for someone to move past him toward the staircase without him noticing? Could they have not only snuck past him, but so quickly that Rick didn't see him either? The other staff members teased them about their apparition sighting, naturally being skeptical. Well, little did John and Rick know, they would have an opportunity to prove themselves....

A few weeks later when they went to close up, they heard footsteps upstairs once again. They thought for sure that it had to be the other staff pulling a trick on them. In order to catch them in the act, they both ran to opposite ends of the room and went up the opposing stairs at the same time.

There was no other way out and one of them would certainly see who it was making the sound. They agreed to stay on the stairs and report to each other what they saw at their ends of the room. Neither of them saw anyone. They called back and forth to each other, trying to figure out how someone might have snuck past them and how very unlikely it would have been, when a dark shape passed by the doorway between them, blocking their view of each other completely. They didn't stick around to investigate. They ran like hell.

"Although apparitions very often look and behave like ordinary human beings (the transparent or grotesque apparitions of legend, though known, are not common), they tend to vanish suddenly, leaving no trace behind; to perform physically impossible feats such as passing through doors or walls; and to move instantaneously from one place to another." (*Handbook of Parapsychology*, 601)

Word spread amongst the staff and they had chosen the name Irving for the ghost (after a former staff member who'd had an unfortunate accident). During a Halloween night when the tour still included the upstairs, half a dozen people saw a grey-haired, balding man behind the bunks. When they pointed him out, he disappeared despite the pursuit of a few people trying to find out who it was.

In 1997 there was a special, summer re-enactment when the organizers stayed in the upper story of Blockhouse 2. One of them had a dog. They say that animals can see and sense things that humans can't. This little cocker spaniel whimpered and yelped, trying to resist going upstairs. When the owner yanked on the leash and brought it upstairs, the dog raced towards the far side of the building closer to Blockhouse 1 as soon as the leash was taken off its neck. The organizers followed the dog to see if it was chasing a mouse or something, but when they caught up to it…the dog was barking and growling at the empty corner.

There have been other reports of footsteps heard from the second story even after it was no longer accessible to tourists, and when there has been no possible way for a human to have been walking around in the corners of the locked areas. But it's not just the upper floor of Blockhouse 2 that is haunted; there are stories about ghosts on the first floor that are just as creepy.

On rainy days, the staff working as guides find themselves with little to do. The fort is such an open area that few tourists come to walk out in the miserable weather. Very often the guides will lean on the doorframes facing the field, bored. As John stood in the doorway, he felt a little tug on the back of his jacket. Although he had been pretty sure there was nobody in the building, he assumed there was someone behind him trying to politely get his attention so that they could exit the building. When he turned around, there was nobody there. Of course, it could have been his imagination. He didn't see anyone by the bunk beds or along the other walls hiding, so he chalked it up to his imagination on a slow day. He went back to leaning on the doorframe and waiting for the rain to pass. After only a few more moments, John felt a tug on the back of his coat again. He turned around quickly, fully expecting to see another bored staff member playing a trick on him to pass the time. Once again he found himself completely alone in the building. At this point, John started to wonder if it was something other than a prank…perhaps it was one of the ghosts of Blockhouse 2. He returned to his position and hoped the little game was over. A third time, his coat was pulled from behind and again, there was nobody there when he spun around. Instead of feeling scared and running out of the building, John simply turned around to the room and called out, "Irving, stop it!" The tugging game ended. It's possible that one of the children who died in that building still wants to play.

Once the upstairs was closed to tourists, there was more activity on the main floor. When the doors slammed shut, possibly because of winds, staff members began to blame "Irving" again, usually out of fun. One day, George continued to open the door that kept slamming shut and when he got tired of going back and forth, he put a heavy bucket of sand that was kept by the wood stove in the way of the door. He jokingly challenged, "Ha! Try to shut the door now, Irving!" The door slammed shut with a crash. After his heart skipped a beat, George decided it was the wind once again. He went to clean up the sand that must have toppled over with the force, but found no mess on the floor. He looked outside thinking the sand had been pushed out, but there was no bucket of sand outside, either. When he turned around to find where the bucket of sand could have gone, he noticed that it was placed neatly in its original position by the wood stove almost twelve feet away from where he placed it.

A woman came to Blockhouse 2 with a lot of historical questions for the tour guide, Mark. While the adults talked, her son went further into the building to play and climbed up on one of the bunk beds. The adults soon noticed that the boy was having a very animated conversation with someone, but there was nobody there. Mark commented on how cute it was that he had an imaginary friend. The woman was confused since her son had never spoken to, or about, an imaginary friend before. She finished asking her questions and when it was time to leave, the little boy didn't want to go. They both went over to where the boy was sitting on the bed to find out what was going on. When Mark asked who he was talking to, the boy plainly answered, "The man."

The little boy described the man to be about the same height as Mark and wearing a red military type of uniform. "He's got the same red coat with the long tails, but the man has got yellow strips on his cuffs and collars instead of green like you do." Those who know British history well enough know that every Regiment had its own colour coding that was usually on their uniform cuffs or collars. Did the little boy know the history of 1812 well enough to know and be able to describe a soldier from that time and from that war specifically? When they asked him what the man was telling him, the boy mentioned that he was very unhappy. He didn't know how he ended up in the Barracks, and didn't know where all of his friends had gone. He was also very confused that most people wouldn't talk to him or even look at him. He didn't like so many people walking through his home, and he wanted them all to go away. The mother finally convinced her son to go, and Mark was left wondering if it was just the tourists — or also the staff — that was not welcome in Blockhouse 2.

"Apparitions of Deceased Persons. Such apparitions may be classed as 'veridical' if either (a) the percipient did not know and had no reason to suspect that the person in question had died, (b) the apparition was of some deceased person not known to the recipient but subsequently recognized him from a photograph or detailed description, or better still picked out by him from a series of photographs or descriptions, or (c) the apparition conveyed some information once known to the deceased person concerned, but previously unknown to the recipient." (*Handbook of Parapsychology*, 604)

A woman once told Kyle after a previous tour, about a curious follower that tagged along with them out of the Barracks. The woman described a young girl of about seven to nine years old with shoulder length, blonde curly hair, wearing a flowing white gown and she was barefoot. While still in Blockhouse 2, the little girl came half way down the stairs to listen to the stories. After a while, she came right down to the first floor near the guide at the bottom of the stairs. When the group had left the warm room, the little girl followed up close to the tour guide. She only went as far as the Officers' Quarters and could go no further, and she was seen running into that building. The little girl's name was Sarahann.

Nobody else on the tour saw the little girl. Kyle wrote, "...there was a certain discrepancy that was present in the woman's story: her description of the girl's hair. There were certainly little girls living in the Barracks historically, and it is just as certain that little girls died in the Barracks. These would have been the children of soldiers however, which would mean that their hair would be either long and tied back or in a braid, or cut very short to prevent fleas, ticks, lice, and other vermin. A soldier's child in the early 1800s would not have worn her hair shoulder length and curly." (*Niagara's Ghosts 2*, 91)

In August of 1996 another staff member, Sonja, saw Sarahann in Blockhouse 2 while Kyle was telling stories. She described a young girl with blondish hair and in light clothing, sitting on a bunk bed swinging her legs back and forth as she listened to the stories. When Kyle walked past her, she disappeared.

Kyle pointed to various parts of the room we were in, and when he was done, we went back outside to continue the tour. I was happy to have the chance to warm up before we walked around the rest of the fort. We headed back towards the far end of Fort George, and I started to feel a little sick to my stomach as we approached the area just behind the Officers' Quarters. I know I didn't eat anything strange, and I'd been feeling fine all day. I thought I could just walk it off and didn't bother mentioning it to G as we followed the lantern in the dark. The sickness just came upon me and this was when Kyle stopped to talk to the group. I had an urge to just keep walking, maybe go back in circles to keep my mind off of the feeling, but I wanted to hear everything and forced myself to stand still. He then told us a story about a psychic who could go no further than that exact point where we stood and had turned back, sensing horrible things from the back

The Powder Magazine (in the forefront).

end of the Fort. I thought it was a strange coincidence that I started feeling sick at that same part of our tour, but ignored it. He pointed out some benches where some other psychics sat in the dark, refusing to go to the back and enter the area that lead towards the tunnel.

We moved on and followed the path down a bit of a hill and around the only original building left in the fort—the powder magazine.

We approached the thick, heavy looking wooden door leading to the tunnel and waited for the iron latch to be unlocked to let us in. The door swung open easily since the hinges were well maintained. I'm one of those people that does not take well to not being able to see where I'm walking. The four foot wide and six and a half foot tall tunnel was very dark and the only light was in Kyle's hand as we entered the musty stone and earth walkway. Luckily, the ground is quite even and I didn't have any difficulty moving forward. We reached the end, just below the Watchtower on the outside of the fort, and everyone tried to crowd in so that they could hear the stories. Another lady and I sat on the wooden stairs right by the barrel that had the lantern on it. Once we were all gathered and ready, Kyle continued.

When the school of psychics went through, two people felt a childlike presence, a little girl lost in this world. They attempted to open a portal to the next world to save her from her frightening existence. Another group of women saw "a small, translucent white hand on the railing of the stairs, or reaching out to pat the guide gently on the head" in Blockhouse 1 (*Niagara's Ghosts 2*, 92). Some have heard a little girl's giggling and other phenomenon, but Kyle remained skeptical about Sarahann until something happened to him while waiting for people to file into the tunnel.

The way that the tunnel is shaped and the way that any outside light would come in makes the entrance and whatever is beyond it very visible even past people's heads (almost like a binocular effect). When Kyle was guiding a ghost tour, there was a thunderstorm that was perfect for telling spooky ghost stories. He was surprised to see someone's child standing out by the entrance instead of coming in. The child stared for a while, paced, and came back, but did not enter the tunnel. Assuming it might be too scary, he looked for a parent to be outside with the child instead of leaving them out there all alone. He asked if anyone was missing a child before any parents panicked, but there was no answer. If the child snuck in and wanted to play a prank, there would be nobody to stop them from shutting and locking the door, trapping everyone inside. He kept an eye out as he continued to talk.

When lightning struck and lit up the sky, the child was not there. He could only see the walls of the powder magazine. As soon as the lightning stopped, he could see the child's form again at the entrance of the tunnel. Another lightning flash—and the child disappeared only to instantly reappear again. It might have been Sarahann. If it was Sarahann, why didn't she enter the tunnel? What was she afraid of?

A woman and her two daughters attended the ghost tour for the first time. As they entered the tunnel, the woman was already feeling uneasy in the darkness. She was with her two little girls, 7 and 9 years of age. She regretted being at the back of the line as the tour guide led the group through the tunnel, and she reached out to grab the girls' little hands and pulled them close before going deeper into the darkness. She tried to lead the older of the two daughters in front of her and pulling the youngest behind, she made her way along the stone pathway when she heard a voice ahead of her. "Mommy, where are you?" It was her youngest daughter. The brave little girl had gone ahead, leaving mom and her older sister to enter the tunnel last. So whose hand was she holding onto behind her as they walked? Sarahann might have needed a little motherly guidance to give her the courage to enter just a little further into the tunnel.

Chris was guiding a tour on Halloween night of 2001. Having a large group that night, Chris backed right up to the wall by the barrel in order to make as much space as he could for everyone to fit in the small area by the landing of the steps. As he was speaking he'd stopped cold in the middle of what he was saying. Since he resumed soon after, nobody thought anything of it until he talked about it later with Meghan who was on security. Someone had grabbed his shoulder. Everyone in the tunnel was in front of him. His back was to the wall and there was no person within arm's reach. It didn't hurt, but it was enough pressure to be an unmistakable hand. Something was trying to get his attention. When Chris got home that night and took off his shirt, the exact spot where his shoulder had been grabbed was bruised. There were three distinct bruises on the front and one on the back in the pattern of three fingers and a thumb.

Most of the time when a person grabs another, the baby finger is not strong enough to make an impression like the other three more dominant fingers or thumb.

Or maybe, the invisible person who grabbed him was missing a finger?

The Octagonal Blockhouse/ Lookout Building the back of the Fort George, the Tunnel leads from inside the fort to the outside building. The steps and barrel where the stories were told were directly underneath this tower.

Mark submitted a story about a time when he was running a tour on Halloween. One of the tourists who was the last to enter had closed the door of the tunnel behind them to preserve the heat. Mark left the group to go back to the entrance to open it back up, and walked back to the group to continue telling the ghost stories. He could hear noises from above in the lookout building, the Octagonal Blockhouse. The rest of the group's attention was on whoever was upstairs rather than on the tour, so he assumed that one of the tourists had snuck up the stairs to check it out and perhaps have a little fun when he wasn't looking. "Okay, the joke's over." He repeated this even though the others assured him that no one had gone up the steps. He climbed to the second landing and peeked at the first floor where he saw a shadowing figure crouched on the floor with knees curled up, tapping their feet on the floor. Still thinking it was one of the tourists, Mark said, "Okay, I can see you, it's time to come down." He got a light handed up to him from below and when he brought it up and said "Okay, I'm not joking…" the light would have fallen on the crouching figure had it not completely disappeared. Mark returned to the group, who were anxiously waiting to hear about what was upstairs. He simply said, "I think it's time to go."

Kyle was still worried about that entrance door closing while we were on the tour. We found out that he had every reason to be a little nervous as he kept an eye on the entrance. On the last night of ghost tours in 1995, people were conjugating at the landing by the barrel when both he and another staff member saw two figures silhouetted at the entrance. The door slammed shut. After a few screams and some nervous laughter, he went to open the door and found nobody who could have closed it. Everyone on the tour was still inside. He came back to continue, but had to talk as loud as he could to be heard over the other unexpected noise. It sounded as if there were people stomping around just above them, slamming doors and marching back and forth. Everyone on the tour was still with him. It was very unlikely that a group of very nimble pranksters could have scaled the ten foot high, spiked palisade that surrounded the Octagonal Blockhouse lookout to get in that way. When Kyle went back at the end of the night to investigate, he found that the entrance to the Octagonal Blockhouse was still properly locked and barred from the inside. Since then, there have been other times and more reports from when the door to the tunnel closed on its own.

So who is it in the tunnel at the back end of Fort George? Some of the answers might date back to 1978 when Margaret Hopkins first visited. When Margaret was exiting the tunnel, she noticed that the electric lights behind her went out. She commented to her friend Darlene that a fuse must have blown and that they should let the staff know about it.

Darlene responded, "What are you talking about? The lights are still on, plain as day." Margaret looked again and saw that she was mistaken. The first two sets of lights were still lit but beyond that a "mass of darkness" blocked the tunnel about fifteen feet from the entrance. "As Margaret watched, three shadowy figures materialized from this 'solid cloud of shadow.' These three male figures, who wore tall hats (she believes they were soldiers from the War of 1812), then began moving towards her and the entrance of the tunnel." As they got closer, she turned to grab her friend and ran away from the entrance as fast as she could. Almost twenty years later, Margaret collected her courage and came back to Fort George and joined the Ghost Tour. When the group approached the tunnel, she was understandably apprehensive, but ventured on through the entrance. After taking only three steps in, she could feel the three beings crowding around her. She stopped in her tracks, turned right around, and waited outside until the rest of the tour joined her again.

On May 13, 2001, Kyle was about to leave the tunnel with a group of people on the tour, when he saw a swirling haze blocking the exit. After a short pause, Kyle decided that the strange hazy area would most likely dissipate as he approached it and decided not to worry and keep on walking. "So in I went stepping through the haze towards the light. Now you know how sometimes you get that shiver that runs from the back of your neck down your spine? That's not what happened. As I stepped through the haze, a chock of cold from the bottom of my spine shot up along my back to the top of my head. But then I was through and out." (*Niagara's Ghosts 2*, 88) Nobody else felt any cold sensations. One of the "regulars" said that they had watched him walk through more than one individual by the entrance before they disappeared.

Is it the three men that are keeping Sarahann out of the tunnel? Are they the only reason why so many people feel a sense of dread when they approach the entrance or walk down the stone path? A couple of stories suggest there might be something more.

Mark, the tour guide, keeps the story of Merritt's Dragoons alive by dressing in an authentic uniform that he had researched and collected himself. (A "Dragoon" used their horses to move them from place to place, but did not ride them while they were fighting. Most, if not all of their fighting was done dismounted using a weapon known as a musketoon in the early days, which was a shortened musket.) Part of this authentic uniform is a suede sabretache — a flat side "purse" or sack that hangs from the belt to the knee. He was involved in the annual battle re-enactment and afterwards cleaned himself up to preserve the unique uniform (especially the suede sabretache). He stayed afterwards with Gord to help close and lock up Fort George. When they entered the tunnel and walked about forty feet in, Mark interrupted his conversation with Gord to apologize for bumping him with his sword. Gord said he wasn't bumped at all. On the way back out, Mark apologized for bumping into him again, and once more Gord was confused. As they were finishing up, both men stopped to listen to what they thought was a growl coming from outside. They couldn't see anything, so they exited and locked up the big wooden door. Gord stopped Mark before they went any further. There was a cougar paw print on his suede sabretache.

Steven and three younger volunteer staff were working in the summer of 2001, and again it was time to go back and start locking up the fort. All four guys walked into the tunnel, and Steven and one of the volunteers stayed at the bottom of the stairs while the other two went up into the blockhouse to make sure everything was clear and set. When they had checked everything out and were ready to come back down the stairs, they stopped. Steven could hear a nervous voice asking where he was. He called back up and said that he was still at the bottom landing and asked what was wrong.

"THERE'S SOMETHING ON THE STAIRS!"

The two staff members at the bottom of the steps were "nearly trampled by the screaming, spinning, leaping mass that thundered down the stairs and onto the floor of the tunnel." (*Niagara's Ghosts 2*, 89) All four guys ran for the exit as fast as they could with a dark shape following behind them. They were bumping into each other and against the walls trying not to be the last one out. Three of the guys flew out of the tunnel and closed the door behind them not realizing there was one more person inside, until there was a thump on the inside of the door and they heard a whimper through the small barred window. They opened the door just a crack to let him out, but when they did, there was an invisible force trying to pull him back into the tunnel. They managed to pull him free, and still screaming, they closed and bolted the door shut before running from the fort altogether.

As I mentioned before, I was sitting on those stairs when I was on the ghost tour with Kyle. When he was done telling his stories while standing at the barrel, we headed back out along the tunnel towards the entrance. He told a few stories about people rushing out and things that they've experienced. I waited to hear someone from the back let out a whimper or scream, or to ask the invisible person beside them not to bump them again, but nothing happened. I don't remember feeling anything myself even though I was sitting on those stairs, no man or animal spirit nudged me, and there were no paw prints left on any of us. All I knew was that I was still feeling sick to my stomach and wanted to get back out into the open air and walk it off. Kyle closed the big wooden door behind us when the whole group had exited, and we walked over to the Gift Shop area.

Of course, it wasn't originally constructed to be a Gift Shop. It was the kitchen that was built next to what was the hospital at the time (now the Artificers' Shop). I thought that if my feeling sick were in any way a psychic feeling, being beside an old hospital would explain it. Medicine as it was practiced in 1812 was not as precise as what we're used to today. Add to the fact that a makeshift hospital in a fort in a time of war was far more rudimentary even for their time. I already knew about some of the medical practices in the early 1800s, but some people found out the hard way.

On a previous tour, there was a very brave young teen who proclaimed that he was not afraid of anything. Before Kyle even had a chance to tell the group any details, the teen looked into the middle window of the Artificer's Shop. He quickly backed away from the window swearing, "OH SHIT… OH SHIT… OH SHIT…" He ran to his mother who held him and tried to calm him down. When he finally stopped swearing and was able to talk about what he saw, he described, "… a person lying on the table, two men holding him down, and someone was sawing at his leg."

If a person had a limb that was damaged beyond repair, it had to be removed so that the person could survive. As the soldiers were brought into the hospital during the War of 1812, many of them had to have limbs removed with a saw as they were held down. There was usually no anesthesia available, and aside from a swig of liquor, these men felt every second of the

A view of the Gift Shop from the back of Fort George.

amputation. In some cases the bone was only cut halfway through with the saw, and they would snap off the limb the rest of the way. When you think about it, that was a much faster way to finish the operation than to continue slowly sawing all the way through. The amount of extreme suffering and death that happened in that building was immense. No wonder a seemingly fearless boy backed away scared after seeing such a sight from the past.

There are a few stories from the Gift Shop as well. If you're in the park during the day, there are public washrooms available in the Gift Shop. Although this is useful information, you should also know to keep your ears peeled while you're in there. A girlfriend of a staff member who was visiting said she'd heard footsteps upstairs. When she told others about it, they too went inside and heard footsteps above them. There's only one problem. There is no second story to this building. Naturally they looked for any kind of animals that might have been crawling on the roof, and found none. Kyle looked further into the history of this building and was able to find an old painting where you can see the Gift Shop and bathrooms, and back then, it did have a second floor.

I could barely listen to the stories. I didn't look in any windows, and I really thought I was going to throw up. Again, I tried to remember what I had eaten, or had to drink that day. Had I spent too much time outside in the sun? The skeptic in me was looking for any reason or cause for my sick feeling. I noticed the crowd moving along and I followed them over to the Officers' Quarters. As soon as I left that area and moved towards the front of the fort again, I felt better. I mean, I instantly felt better. I no longer felt sick at all, and there wasn't even a lingering queasiness. It was just gone and I felt great. I wanted to be a good tourist and stay with the group, but a large part of me wanted to walk back and forth between the two areas to see if the sick feeling came and went again as quickly and consistently each time. Maybe the next time I go, I'll try it. I could think of no logical explanation as to why I became sick and then suddenly not, and even though I am a believer in science, things like this make me also believe in what science has yet to prove. I tried to put it all behind me and reflect on it later as I wanted to hear the new stories by the Officers' Quarters.

In the middle of the fort grounds is a large yellow building surrounded by a white picket fence in front. Usually the men who lived in the Officers' Quarters paid their way into the position from simply being enlisted men in the British Army. Any officers that were older or had more money bought their own homes in the surrounding area. This created more of a partying atmosphere than a serious officers' headquarters. Their beds, furniture, food, drinks, and cigars were the best in the fort. Perhaps that was one of the reasons why some never wanted to leave?

I'm pretty sure Kyle started with the story about the haunted mirror, and we each took turns walking up to the windows to peek in and see if we could see "The Woman." She's usually seen in profile and described to be a young woman with dark, curly hair. Reports from tourists that date back over twenty years include the exact same description of this woman, but she's not always in the mirror. She has also been seen sitting in front of the mirror and even mistaken for another staff member in costume.

One little girl about the age of five or six described the person that she saw in the Sitting Room. The pretty lady in a "Cinderella dress had long, dark (not black) slightly curly hair, which she had been brushing...using a large white and silver hairbrush" that looked broken. The woman held the brush in her palm and there was a strap across her hand to keep it in place, which is exactly how a hairbrush would have looked back then. Of course, a child would not know this historically correct detail.

Many of the sightings could have been strange lighting and reflections from the windows, or perhaps another person on the tour seems to appear in the mirror. Kyle had never seen her, and I was staring for as long as I could to see her. What eventually convinced

Kyle was the report from a Fort George staff member who decided to come along on the tour at night. At the end, when everyone was telling their stories, he waited for the others to finish and leave before commenting on the great job. "But the best part was how you had Dan and Jenn inside the Officers' Quarters with their period clothes on as the tour went by outside!" Kyle had to tell him that there are no staff members in the buildings at night during the tours other than the tour guides and security, and they are not in costume.

Sometimes the woman is seen brushing her hair, looking slightly annoyed at the tour going by, or even walking around outside of the building. In a place that was inhabited by men, why would there be a ghost of a woman? The mirror predates the War of 1812, possibly from 1790, and was not a part of the historical furnishings of Fort George. When the mirror was moved in, did the young woman come with it? This is one possible theory.

There is also a piano in the Officers' Quarters. A pianoforte to be exact. The one that is in the Sitting Room now is a reproduction of the antique piano, right down to the reverse coloured keys since ivory was more expensive. There have been many times, during the night and even in the middle of the day, when the pianoforte has been heard playing when there was nobody in the building. Sometimes when walking by, an entire party could be heard with the pianoforte playing, singing and talking. All of the sounds vanish suddenly when anybody enters to check out what's making all the noise. One staff member who was a talented pianist decided to play some songs to entertain the visitors. About halfway through her performance, she discovered that the keys that she played were not making the music that was coming out of the piano.

Another tour guide named Wendy made the mistake of calling Queen Charlotte, Queen Mary, and made a comment about her not-so-attractive appearance. She then felt a strange feeling of being moved down to the ground, not tripping or falling backwards, but as if she was being laid down on the ground. She got up nervously and tried to act as if it was all a part of her performance and continued the tour. When she was later talking to the security staff about the incident, "He described that it looked like I had been actually picked up about 3 or 4 inches off the ground, and laid flat down. Even my cape was sort of neatly caught under me. It seemed that my feet actually left the ground." She made sure she always used the proper name of Queen Charlotte from that day on, and discreetly asked for forgiveness. She did not experience anything strange for the rest of that season.

We moved on and started to head back towards the front gate. As we passed by Blockhouse 1 again, we were told one more story about a former staff member on his last night. William Foster was a believer in science, not imagination, but when he heard the footsteps behind him on the path as he passed Blockhouse 1, he started to get nervous. He'd lagged far behind the tour and nobody else was around to hear, or to make those footsteps behind him. As the steps got closer, they also became faster until the unseen person was sprinting right at him. Too late to run away, William fell to the ground and threw his arms up over his face to defend himself. He screamed out in terror, attracting the attention of the tour who came back to see if he was okay. As they ran towards him, his "attacker" ran in the opposite direction, not back into the Blockhouse, but between the two Blockhouses and into the shadows. Foster's face had turned white and he was badly shaken, but he had to go back into the fort to lock up after the tour. He saw the figure again in the window of Blockhouse 1, smiling and taunting him with a wave. He later said to Kyle, "...you have to promise me that you will never take a group into that building...because there are some things in Fort George that don't like us in their fort."

Outside the walls there are just as many ghosts walking around the park grounds. On one ghost tour, Chris I., from St. Catherine's, was talking to a psychic named Susan, who was able to see an astonishing thirty to forty soldiers walking around outside of the front entrance. Most of them looked injured in some way, and weren't really doing anything, just walking around in an unorganized fashion. She pulled herself and Chris away from the rest of the group and tucked away in some trees. Two of the ghosts had noticed that the psychic could see them and turned to start following them. The ghosts stopped about ten feet short of them, watched them for a few minutes, and returned to their group. Chris decided to go and get his camera to try to capture some, or all of them on film. He walked out to the area where Susan told him where they were and when he was surrounded, she yelled out to him that..."Six or seven are encircling you! One of them is reaching out to touch you!" Chris felt nothing. She then told him that another soldier walked right though him, and although he felt a pain between his shoulders, he chalked it up to the spinal surgery (years ago) just acting up again. When he was told that one of the soldiers had climbed onto his back, Chris had had enough and started to walk back towards the group. As he got closer, even Kyle could see something around him, and Chris stopped dead in his tracks totally freaked out. He decided his best course of action was to just talk to the ghost directly. "If there's a spirit of a soldier, from the War of 1812, stationed at Fort George, who is on my back, sir, I apologize that I do not know your name, rank or regiment, that I might address you properly. I am leaving the fort and I am going home and I do not wish to take you with me. I feel the fort is where you belong,

The gates of Fort George.

so I would please ask that you get off my back." (*Niagara's Ghosts 2*, 125) The soldier got off his back and returned to his group. Nothing showed up in Chris' pictures.

In July of 1995, there was a séance in the Barracks. Some of the staff members remembered hearing a child laughing close to the stairwell, but nothing else out of the ordinary happened. When they left, one of the staff members saw a soldier at the front gate waiting for everyone to leave. Another staff member saw a male figure standing by one of the cannons outside of the gates. When they arrived to work the next morning, there was no man to be found, of course, but there was also no cannon. Those cannons weigh about four thousand pounds and no person could move them on their own.

Could the ghostly artillerist have taken his weapon along with him?

One of the cannons at the front gates of Fort George that weighs close to 4,000 pounds.

Sarahann has also made an appearance outside of the Fort George walls. Two people came out into the parking lot where they could see two of the female guides from the first tour walking ahead of them. Between the two guides, they saw a little blond girl walking so closely to them she could have been holding their hands. Disappointed that there were no actors dressed as ghosts on their tour, they approached the two female guides to ask why there was a difference between the two tours. The little girl completely vanished, leaving the witnesses completely shocked.

If you ever visit St. Mark's Anglican Church on Byron Street, you might be able to find the grave of Sarahann in the cemetery (along the path at the side by making a left at a leaning tree). It says:

> "In Memory of SARAHANN
> Daughter of HANNAH and
> THOMAS B. TRACEY,
> Troop Serjeant Major In the kings Dragoon-Guards.
> Who died On the 19th of July, 1840
> In the 7th year of her Age."

After doing some research, Kyle noticed that the dates did not match up with the War of 1812, but rather with the time when William Lyon Mackenzie led a rebellion against Upper Canada. With a new military presence in Niagara-on-the-Lake, the old fort was used for a detachment of a cavalry. Thomas Tracey's association with that cavalry and his daughter's name being mentioned by the psychic are incredible coincidences. It does, however, explain that a soldier's child in 1812 would not have had curly, shoulder-length hair, but a soldier's daughter in 1840 definitely would have and it was very fashionable to do so.

We picked up some Tim Horton's brand coffee to be sure we were awake enough to drive back home. It was too dark to make any notes in my notebook, and it's too hard to read jumbled car writing anyway. I sat back and tried to go over all of the stories again in my head so that I would remember as many details as possible. When I thought about the stories in Blockhouse 2, I remembered my cell phone beeping saying that I had a message. I really did have my phone on and with me all day before the tour and there was no way I could have missed a call. I turned my phone back on and the little icon was in the corner. I checked voice messages, and there were none. I checked text messages, and there were none. When I got back to the main menu, the little icon was gone. I've never had this happen before or since. Was it a coincidence that my phone chose that night to do something weird? Was it Sarahann or another one of the children playing with the electronics? It's not enough for me to tell you that ghosts do in fact exist because my phone acted up, but I thought it was pretty cool and it made me smile.

Many thanks again to Kyle Upton. Not only for sharing all of his stories and his book with me, but also for running a fantastic Ghost Tour of Fort George. There are many more stories in and around Fort George that will make your hair stand on end. I highly recommend that you go on a tour if you can and buy Kyle's book to read about all of the stories he's discovered over the years. I know I'll be going back for another tour. Perhaps I'll see something more the next time I go?

Maid of the Mist

http://www.maidofthemist.com/en/

The American (forefront) and Canadian (background) Maid of the Mist.

When you go down to Niagara Falls, you will see one of the tourist boats that take you closer to the bottom of the Falls, *The Maid of the Mist*. All of the passengers are wearing rain slickers or ponchos, and some manage to pull out their waterproof cameras. When I was a little kid, I had seen the Maid of the Mist tours, but I didn't know that there was a ghostly story behind the name.

The *Maid of the Mist I* was launched on May 27, 1846 as a means of transportation across the river. When the

International Bridge was completed, the ferry was no longer needed. In order to continue making any money, it had to become a tourist boat instead. *The Maid of the Mist II* was launched on July 14, 1854. Propelled by a steam paddle wheeler with a single smoke stack, this boat was much larger than the original at seventy-two feet long. This ship was sold due to a financial crisis and the impending American Civil War. Captain Joel Robinson had to deliver the boat to the new owners through tumultuous waters.

"Captain Robinson had great difficulty breaking the Maid of the Mist from the grip of the Whirlpool before challenging the final leg of this dangerous trip through the dreaded Devil's Hole Rapids. As the boat escaped the grips of the Whirlpool, Captain Robinson did the best he could to hold a course through the center of the channel with his badly damaged vessel. The three mile journey through the rapids and the whirlpool was successful except for losing the smoke stack. Captain Robinson had accomplished something no one had done before and thought impossible." (www.iaw.com/~falls/devil_frame.html)

The journey frightened the Captain into retirement and he died two years later.

The newest *Maid of the Mist VII* that you will find taking tourists into the water today was officially launched into service on Friday, July 11, 1997.

I found the legend of a native girl who ran from a hateful marriage and chose death instead by riding her canoe over the Falls. "She rode her canoe over the Falls but was saved at the last moment by the Native God He-No, the Thunderer. He carried her to his cave, which is hidden by the mist of the Falls, but from time to time you can see her reflection in the water as she peers out through the deluge." (*Ghost Waters*, 96-97)

Another more traditional version of this story is about a girl named Lelawala. Legend has it that when Indian tribes were inexplicably dying, they started to send offerings of fruit over the Falls in canoes to appease the gods, God Hinum and his two sons. When there was no improvement, they decided to sacrifice their most beautiful woman every year and send her over the Falls. Lelawala, the daughter of the Chief, was placed into a canoe with the fruit offerings and sent over the Falls. Hinum's sons caught her and she agreed to become the wife of one of them under one condition; they had to save her people. They told her about the snake that would come out once a year and poison the water that the tribes had been drinking and they went back to warn the tribes as promised, and told them how to kill the snake. On the night when the snake appeared the Indian braves did exactly what they were told would work and used their spears, sending it back to the edge of the Falls where it died leaving its body in a horseshoe shape. It remains a horseshoe shape to provide a reminder that the Gods are still protecting the people from evil spirits. Lelawala returned to the cave of the God Hinum, where she reigns as the Maid of the Mist.

Until you can actually get down to Niagara Falls yourself and hear the thunder and roar of the Falls from the Maid of the Mist, you can look online for videos that other tourists have taken. (I tried to get a couple as well.) You will see a lot of people having to wipe their camera lenses and ponchos flying into the corners of the shots. There might be the sound of an announcer on the tour over the speakers, if you're lucky enough to hear it at all over the booming water and whipping wind sounds. When you do get a chance to visit the Falls, you can board the *Maid of the Mist* on the American side at the entrance to the Observation Tower or on the Canadian side at the bottom of Clifton Hill at the Maid of the Mist Landing.

G and I were able to get down to the Falls and take the tour on the *Maid of the Mist*. We had crossed over to the American side first and we were able to find parking for ten dollars about a block from the water. After a short walk through the park, we got to the Observation Tower and bought our tickets. G remembered going years ago with a class and he told me it would take a while standing in line before boarding. As it turned out, we went straight from buying the tickets to a two minute elevator wait, to picking up the ponchos and about a five minute wait before we saw the boat coming back to

The American Maid of the Mist tour as seen from the top of the Observation Tower.

pick up the next load of passengers. It was one of the most efficient tourist attractions we'd ever seen. During our short wait, we could see across to the Canadian Maid of the Mist dock and it appeared to move just as quickly.

When we boarded, we were able to get right up at the front and off we went. A recorded voice came over the speakers, but it was soon difficult to hear what they were saying over the roar of the water. I tried to take a short video of the American Falls with my digital camera and after about thirty seconds I had to tuck it away before it got too wet. The water came crashing down onto the rocks and it looked like a painting in motion. I had decided not to use the hood on the poncho as it was restricting my view and flapping around my camera and my hair and part of my sleeve got wet trying to take pictures. Since you don't really get wet from the waist down, I would suggest gathering as much of the loose poncho as you can and tucking it either between your legs or maybe in your pockets because it blows up and around you quite a bit. There were hundreds of seagulls sitting or flying around between the American Falls and the Horseshoe Falls. As we got closer to the Canadian side the water became much more tumultuous and the boat started to rock a little. The immensity of the Falls and the power of the water are truly hypnotic and very intimidating. I took some still shots and, as we got closer to the mist, I tried to take another short video. The water from the "mist" was coming at us like rain flying sideways and G told me that if I wrecked the camera he would kill me, so again I had to put it back in its case.

There was some talk around us about some of the people who have gone over the Falls (as you'll read about in the next chapter) and I tried to imagine exactly what flavour of crazy you'd have to be to leap off a mountain of water one hundred and seventy feet high and over two thousand feet wide, into a meat-grinding blender made of six hundred thousand gallons of water and rocks. We felt very small — and very breakable — next to this incredible wonder of the world. We sat below the Falls for a little while as the boat idled, watching the water around us. We were trying to see through the mist, and watching the water tumble over the edge is truly amazing.

Tours cannot run during the winter months when the ice proves to be too dangerous, so please check with the website to see the updated information and more about prices and group rates. Take your family on the half hour tour and make sure you look extra carefully at the mist at the bottom of the Falls. Perhaps you will be able to see the legendary Maid of the Mist.

Two boats taking turns their way into the mist at the bottom of the Horseshoe Falls, as seen from the top of the Observation Tower.

Part Two

Death

"The water has a certain magnetism... for some people. They feel an urge to jump and they have to walk away from it before this overcomes them and they do jump in."
— *Leo Donovan, Homicide Chief,*
Buffalo Police Department, 1985

"The goal of all life is death."

— *Sigmund Freud*

Dark Waters Calling

Freud said that all human behaviour was motivated by subconscious instincts, or drives. Our sexual drive and instinct for life keeps us in forward motion. We have all heard about Freud's precarious theories about sex drives and how he interpreted dreams. The primal need to have sex and procreate, to keep our existence strong throughout history, and our need for love is a very strong drive that can make people do some crazy things. But there was another theory that Freud had that was not accepted as openly. William McDougall, an English psychologist who was sympathetic to most of Freud's ideas, said that it was his "most bizarre monster of all his gallery of monsters." He was talking about the Death Instinct.

The death instinct is our need to make everything still, to stop the pain, to be satisfied, to be at peace, and find the end. Freud believed that we all have a subconscious wish to die. In his book, *Beyond the Pleasure Principle*, he introduces the idea that in life we seek to restore an ancient state of existence that preceded life itself. He even mentions the tendency for people to try to find Nirvana, the Buddhist notion of ultimate tranquility. It refers to non-existence, nothingness, the void, and the goal of Buddhist philosophy. Perhaps it is in search of that tranquility that so many people are drawn to Niagara Falls, and perhaps the hypnotic power of the water brings out that death instinct. It might be true...at least for daredevils and people with suicidal tendencies.

"Fixation to (past) traumas and the 'compulsion to repeat.' ... By 1920 Freud had come to recognize certain classes of neurotic symptoms as involving fixations to, and compulsive repetitions of, traumatic events." (*Freud Biologist of the Mind*, 396)

For some, they are trying to reach a state of peace and stillness, or escape from stimulation using alcohol or drugs. For others it can be satisfied by losing themselves in a good book or sleeping more. In the most extreme cases, the release sought is the ultimate escape, death. Life is a constant struggle, we need breaks. There are some people who don't know how to find or take those necessary breaks in life and strive to cheat death, or achieve death.

I don't personally think that everyone who has ever attempted going over the Falls in a barrel actually had a death wish, or were playing out their death instinct. Thrill seekers and daredevils are out there for the rush, for the attention and money, and to look death in the eye and laugh. I think they really wanted to live life to the extreme and they wanted to conquer their fears.

There are certain feelings that come to us when we are scared. Our hearts race, our stomachs flip a few times, we breathe faster, and we sweat. That could all happen for some people after simply seeing a scary movie or riding on a roller coaster. Knowing that you've come out of the theatre okay, or survived the roller coaster gives us a sense of accomplishment. Our senses have been bombarded in ways we're not used to in our regular daily lives and we are forced to face some of our fears. We emerge victorious!

I love roller coasters, and I've watched people get off the rides with nervous smiles on their faces, or even giggling. Some riders cheer and hoot and holler about how cool the ride was and run back into line, others just look sick and hate the whole experience. I could say the same thing about some people emerging from horror movies at the theatres. Some people just avoid those experiences altogether, and feel no need to conquer, feel the rush, or face their fears, thank you very much. But if you're like me, you're rushing back in line to do it all again.

G and I both love a really scary horror movie. We like to see if the tourist "haunted houses" can scare us. (We've been through both Screamers and Nightmares in Niagara Falls.) We love roller coasters, the bigger the better. We've even been parachuting, a story I love to tell friends from time to time. Some people just have a really intense curiosity about the "dark side" of life and need to know what happens outside of our own safe boundaries. Some children believe their parents when they're told it would be "very bad" to put their fingers in the electrical sockets; other children need to know what it feels like. That "very bad" sometimes needs to be experienced and not simply dismissed. (Heh, yeah, I did that as a kid, too.) Perhaps we're born with the curiosity or a daring side.

Men and women who thrive on the uncertainty and the intensity associated with activities that most people consider to be frightening, are called "Type T" or thrill seeking personalities. Generally higher in men than in women, the thrill seeking drive peaks in the late teens and early twenties, and gradually declines with age (along with levels of testosterone). Finding a way to take care of some of those drives even at an early age can be very important for the release of stress and anxiety. Halloween is another harmless example of a release where children get to dress up and escape behind a mask, feel the thrill of being someone or something else (a monster!), and get to be scared or scare their friends. Of course, not all kids who like Halloween grow up to be thrill seekers, and not all thrill seekers live without boundaries. However, there are a special breed of daredevils who really push the limits of both nature and their own physical abilities. Niagara Falls is a massive force of nature to be messing with. At what point does thrill seeking become simply recklessness? Where do you draw the line between being a daredevil and having a death wish?

> "Murder, suicide, accident. The dead gather in the gorge and rise at the tour boat docks below the falls, in the Whirlpool, or as far away as Lake Ontario. Tragedies witnessed by thousands often result in no body being recovered, while many corpses surface that cannot be identified. In winter and spring, the ice grinds human bodies into limbless torsos. The capricious currents often hold the dead for weeks before releasing them...' (Captain Joseph DeMarco of the New York State Police) witnessed many tragedies in his forty-four years of police work at the Niagara Reservation. He suggested that the Falls claim from four to twelve victims each year." (*Journeys to the Brink of Doom*, 157)

The Onguiaarhas and Senecas believed powerful spirits ruled over Niagara Falls. Some say Hihnon, the Seneca Thunder God, lives there, and others say that there are two gods, Hihnon, and an evil serpent spirit that demands at least four human sacrifices each year. The Indians believed that the evil demon was Tawiscara, the Huron Spirit of Evil, and I'll summarize the legend a

little bit. Ataentsic was told by her father that she was to
go down to the world and marry the "Chief Who Owns
the Earth" whose hut was beside the "big tree of heaven."
They married, but when he saw that she was already with
child, he became furious and jealous of the Fire Dragon.
Ataentsic and her daughter, Breath of Wind, were cast
into the abyss and landed on earth. When Breath of
Wind grew older and paired with the Master of Winds,
they had twins. Loskeha and Tawiscara hated each
other, and fought before they were born, causing their
mother's death. Tawiscara persuaded his grandmother
that Loskeha alone had caused their mother's death. So
she cast him out, knowing it was a lie. Loskeha created
mankind. Tawiscara tried to imitate him to gain favour,
but only succeeded in producing monsters, and in the end
was sent into exile by his brother. (They correspond to
Osiris and Set.) Regardless of the motives behind suicide,
daredevilry or accidents, Tawiscara comes for his four
sacrifices every year at Niagara Falls...

Suicide

"The Roar of the water became overpowering. It seemed to be drawing and inviting me. And then everything went blank. I remembered nothing until I woke up in the hospital hours later." — *Ellen King, 1946, after being rescued before going over the American Falls*

"For about half an hour more I continued to watch the rolling waters and then I felt a slight dizziness and a creeping sensation came over me — that sensation arising from strong excitement, and the same, probably, that occasions the bird to fall into the jaws of the snake. This is a feeling which, if too long indulged in, becomes irresistible, and occasions a craving desire to leap into the flood of rushing waters. It increased upon me every minute; and retreating from the brink, I turned my eyes to the surrounding foliage, until the effect of the excitement had passed away." — *Captain Frederick Marryat, Diary in America, 1839*

Suicide is something that cannot be overlooked when we talk about death in Niagara Falls. Often we like to think that it might have been an accident, but in some cases there is absolutely no question about the person's intent. To many, plunging themselves into the water might seem to be an almost romantic way to die, but when we consider the power of the Falls and what it can do to a human body, it is definitely one of the most gruesome. Usually, hands, arms, legs and heads are ripped from the torso, along with most or all of the clothing, and found days later completely mangled.

I am not writing this chapter lightly. This is an extremely serious issue coupled with the dangers of a crushing Niagara Falls. There are many people in our lives who have suicidal thoughts and might never talk about them, and hopefully, will never act on them. Others make threats and some even go as far as to make attempts, only to change their minds when the reality of death is upon them. It is a permanent solution to a temporary problem.

"Most suicidal thinkers don't want to die; they just want their feelings to change or go away. Every single feeling we experience eventually does change – with or without any help from us. They never stay the same or at the same intensity." (*How I Stayed Alive When My Brain Was Trying To Kill Me*, 3-4)

The chance of surviving a trip over Niagara Falls is minimal, and the chance of someone changing their minds is a very likely, and very tragic, possibility. When some young suicide survivors were asked what was going through their minds right before they almost died, they all answered the same way, "I wanted to change my mind."

Nelson and Galas write, "Faced with the certainty of their own death, most said they suddenly realized their problems weren't so big that somehow they couldn't be solved. Their problems weren't so bad that somehow they couldn't find a way to survive them. In that second before they almost died, they knew they wanted to live." (*The Power to Prevent Suicide*, 12)

Most suicidal people are not mentally ill, they are just struggling with the present emotional and physical difficulties life handed them at the time that seem insurmountable. Very often, people who threaten or try to commit suicide just want to be saved. Saved from themselves or their lives, they do not necessarily want life to end. This is why it is important to recognize warning signs.

Listen to suicide threats and take them seriously, watch for sudden changes in behaviour (including sudden happiness since things will be "all over soon"), giving away possessions, tying up all loose ends and making sure everything is in order, or uncharacteristic aggression or risk taking. The person might feel unlucky, hopeless or helpless, or they might withdraw and become disinterested. Many people who are stopped from following through on one suicidal attempt, never make another.

Preventable Canoe Accident

The Niagara Courier reported the story about Mr. J. McMurry on August 27, 1851. He had been working all day selling vegetables and after work he became considerably drunk. On his way back home to the American side in his canoe, he fell asleep and started to drift towards Goat Island. He was seen asleep right up until he was hitting the first breakers. He jumped up and grabbed the oars and tried to paddle two or three times before the canoe fell into the rapids and broke into pieces. Had he been sober, he could have saved himself. He was never seen again.

I know this wasn't a typical suicide, but I consider this to be more than just an unfortunate accident. It was preventable. Perhaps McMurry was so used to the canoe ride from the American side to the Canadian side and back, that he took it for granted and became careless. To me, this is no different from getting in a car and heading for the familiar strip of highway while intoxicated.

Goodbye, Captain

A former ship's captain and marine surveyor, John Jones, had been in poor health and could not work. After a year of unemployment, he fell into a deep depression that worried his family and friends. When they consulted the doctors, they decided that he needed a change from the New York City life and taking him back to his family in Kansas seemed like the best solution. He agreed under one condition: they had to go sightseeing at Niagara Falls first. When they arrived after a long train ride, they enjoyed dinner and went down to Prospect Park. When they came to an unfenced area on the way to Goat Island, John yelled out over the raging water, "Goodbye!" and leapt into the rapids. His body was found in the Whirlpool eight days later on September 16, 1875.

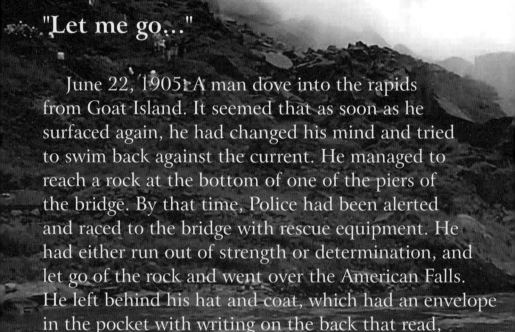

"Let me go..."

June 22, 1905: A man dove into the rapids from Goat Island. It seemed that as soon as he surfaced again, he had changed his mind and tried to swim back against the current. He managed to reach a rock at the bottom of one of the piers of the bridge. By that time, Police had been alerted and raced to the bridge with rescue equipment. He had either run out of strength or determination, and let go of the rock and went over the American Falls. He left behind his hat and coat, which had an envelope in the pocket with writing on the back that read, "I can stand the aches and pains no longer, I fear I shall never be well. Let me go before I lose my mind entirely." (*Journeys to the Brink of Doom*, 20)

Hanging On After Jumping

August 28, 1955: Robert Persons took his wallet out of his pocket and placed it on the ground before climbing up over the fence and dropping himself into the rapids in front of the American Falls. After an anonymous call came in almost five hours later, firefighters descended in slings where they found Parsons desperately hanging on to a rock with water crashing down on him. Most of his clothes had been ripped off and he had a deep cut on his head. He assured the rescuers that he was okay when they pulled him up using thirty-five foot slings. He died when they reached safe ground at Prospect Point.

The rocks alongside the American Falls where Robert Persons hung on for dear life.

Family Mystery

My own family also has a mysterious story from the past. Years ago I'd heard that my father had an aunt who went over Niagara Falls and died. Nobody is sure why, and her siblings would never talk about the incident. Apparently, she had taken her two young daughters to the Falls for a day trip and they're not sure if her falling into the water was an accident or not. My Dad's younger cousin has also heard the story, but never found out any details. When she went to ask her uncle, she didn't get very far:

> "I did know that we had an Aunt that went over the Falls but I don't know the details — my father never spoke about it and I didn't know about it until I was older. I can ask (my aunt) if she knows any of the details. All I really know is that she was married and had two little girls at the time. I've often wondered why she did it and if anyone saw her or if her body was ever found. If (my aunt) knows anything I'll let you know." (In the following email she writes…) "I haven't spoken to (my aunt) but I did ask my uncle because I thought if anyone knew it would be him. He said he would let me know when I was older. I asked him how much older I would have to be and he said much older and if he kicked the bucket first the story would go down the drain with him. I don't think he wanted to tell me. Maybe your Dad would have better luck since he's older than me."

My father had heard about the story from one of his friends years ago and when he went to check with my Grandfather it was simply confirmed that the story was true, and said nothing more. Perhaps there are some family secrets best left forgotten.

Sad Sara

Let's not forget the people that suicide leaves behind. The loved ones who want nothing more than to save the lives of the depressed and downtrodden. Some are even willing to sacrifice their own lives to save others from going over the Falls. A particular story touched me and I wonder if today's knowledge of depression would have helped put things in perspective in 1909.

Sara Cohen of Buffalo had just given birth to a son, her third child. Simply labeled as melancholia, her extreme despondency would now be understood as serious postpartum depression. Unable to take care of her children, her husband Louis grew scared for her and sent for her mother in England. When her mother refused to come to America, it intensified her depression even further. At one point, neighbours had to intervene and take a butcher knife away from Sara and called Louis to come home from work to calm her down.

Louis thought it might be a good idea to take the family on a vacation to visit their friends, the Rosens, and stay for a week in Niagara Falls. For a few days, it seemed to work and Sara was in better spirits, but the depression came back. Mrs. Rosen decided to take Sara to Prospect Park to lighten her mood, but to no avail. The very next day, June 6, Sara wanted to go back and visit the Falls again. Louis told her it wasn't a good idea since she'd already been there, but he eventually gave in and both families went to Prospect Park. They walked from Goat Island over to Three Sisters Islands and Sara seemed to be in a pleasant state of mind, and made pleasant conversation. On the way back from Angeline Island, Sara stopped and gave her diamond ring to her husband claiming that it was too loose for her finger. She looked upriver and asked if she could get a better view by going through some trees and brush on the island. The two adults left the children behind with their friends. Sara asked Louis to take her watch and chain, but he insisted she keep her belongings. Instead of arguing with him further, she jumped in.

Louis ran in after her and grabbed her by the waist, but the momentum carried them both into the water. As he gripped her, he screamed for help. She slipped from his grasp and hit a rock about fifty feet from where the families waited for them before she disappeared under the green water. Louis managed to grab her by the hand while his own feet were wedged in the rocks in shoulder-high water. The current prevented him from pulling her in, and it shoved her under a log. He fought for over ten minutes to pull her out before losing all of his strength and nearly drowning himself. When rescuers arrived they found him still holding her hand even though he knew she was dead. They pulled Louis Cohen to shore and gave him warm clothing, but he insisted they go back and find his wife. He told them exactly where to look, under the log where he'd left her. They found her swirling in an eddy not far from the brink of the Horseshoe Falls, and they retrieved her body before she fell over the edge. He did everything he possibly could to save her.

Fate Frowned Upon Them

There are some relationships that are disastrous in so many ways, it's hard to tell if the odds were stacked against them or if things just got too complicated to figure out. Sometimes when people reach out for help, or try to fix their problems, things only get worse. Life gets harder and harder to endure.

Sadie Hawkins had asked for a divorce when she caught her first husband cheating on her. She moved to Silver Creek, just outside of Buffalo where her father owned a store. It was there that she met Theodore Stewart, fell in love, and despite her previous divorce he asked her to marry him. Her new husband and her father made a great team and the more they worked together, the more prosperous they became. Everything seemed to be going well until Sadie became ill. She suffered with bouts of depression for three years before deciding to get some help from the very successful, Dr. Howie.

Howie had moved from Drummondville, Ontario to Silver Creek with his wife and five children only a few years before in 1875. He was a wonderful father and husband, until he met Sadie. She was beautiful and he fell in love with her right away. He used his position as her doctor to seduce her, and she accepted and returned his advances. Their romance lasted three years before Mrs. Howie, a smart and educated woman, grew suspicious when Sadie's visits became more and more frequent. Dr. Howie paid less attention to his family, and even his practice, as he began to drink more and mistreat his wife. Rumours started to fly, and he made a last ditch effort to straighten things out. In

1881 Howie moved his family and practice to Forestville, five miles away. He tried to break off his ties with Sadie, but she traveled to Forestville when she needed more treatment for her depression. As soon as they got to his examination room, they started making love. Before they could finish, Mrs. Howie broke into the room to confront them. She left after a few words and a few blows, only to return a few moments later to catch them in continued lovemaking. She struck them both in the face with a broomstick and her husband punched her down and started to kick her before she got away.

Mrs. Howie went directly to Sadie's husband in Silver Creek and told him everything. They both filed for divorce. Sadie went to stay with her brother in Buffalo and tried to restart her life, but on July 7, 1881 she disappeared. Dr. Howie stayed at home, and his wife would have been able to forgive him if he could just stay away from Sadie. That seemed to be far too difficult for him and on July 6, he said he was going on a business trip to Pennsylvania.

A "Mr. and Mrs. E. W. Gilbert of Rome" checked into a hotel in Niagara Falls, New York. Each of them wrote letters to their spouses. He wrote to make sure the children were going to be taken care of, and she wrote to her faithful and kind husband to ask for forgiveness and tell him that she had lost all interest in life. A man named Max Amberg saw the couple leaving the post office on the morning of the 8th, and watched them walk arm in arm towards Prospect Park. They found her shawl, and her purse and parasol were left behind.

Sadie's body was recovered on July 12th. Her neck and arm were broken and the body was almost unrecognizable once the water and sun had done their worst. It wasn't until July 14th when they discovered Howie's body below the Falls with two broken legs. On July 14th, both families came to collect the remains of their loved ones, and were appalled at the business-like manner in which they were treated by the coroners who routinely collected bodies from the Falls.

Please, Find Help

If you know someone who might be suicidal, there are things you can do that will help, and possibly save their lives. First of all, take them seriously. If you feel that someone is just crying out for attention, see it as a very desperate cry that probably runs deeper than you realize. Listen to them, and get them to talk about their plan. Find out when and how they plan on committing suicide, and decide how lethal their plans are. Some methods such as jumping into Niagara Falls are more lethal because there is no turning back, and no hospital that can save them. Let them know you want to help, and if you can, find professional help. Pull them out of the dark tunnel, because they can't see the light anymore.

If you are suicidal, please, talk to someone. Find someone you trust and tell them you need help. The National Suicide Prevention Lifeline is a 24-hour, toll-free suicide prevention service available to anyone in suicidal crisis. 1-800-273-TALK (8255), http://www.suicidepreventionlifeline.org

Deadly Accidents

They didn't set out to tempt fate, they did not purposely put themselves in harm's way. It was just an accident. Unfortunately, any accidents in and around Niagara Falls often prove to be deadly.

Avery's Barge

A barge was anchored to the East of Goat Island in Niagara River. Three men who were working on it decided to go to shore in a row boat on the afternoon of July 16, 1853. The current was stronger than usual, and much faster than they expected. One of their oars broke. The small boat entered the American Rapids and as they were swept downstream, the boat capsized. Two of the men immediately went over the American Falls and died. The third man, Samuel Avery, was able to grab the roots of a tree that were sticking out from a large rock not far from Chapin Island. The water was so loud nobody was able to hear his shouts for help. He hung on to those roots in the cold, fast water all night long. It wasn't until the next morning when some tourists noticed him and called for help. Boats and rafts were released from Bath Island Bridge, but none got close enough for him to reach. They also tried tethering a boat to the bridge and tried to lead it more carefully towards him. It reached Avery successfully, and he was able to climb in. As soon as he was in the small boat and they tried to pull him back, it too, capsized right away and tossed him back into the rushing water. Having no strength left, Avery threw his hands up in the air in surrender and screamed before being sent backwards over the brink of the American Falls.

The Eve of Wedded Bliss

On July 4, 1873, the day before they were to get married, eighteen year old Margaret Rollinston and twenty year old John Emerson decided to sail the upper Niagara River. They departed from Chippawa in a small boat named the Dreadnaught. After making a horrible mistake in navigating, the couple ended up in the Canadian Rapids and died. Margaret's body was recovered fifteen miles from the Horseshoe Falls in Youngstown, wearing only a gold ring and shoes with few injuries to her body. Two days later, Emerson's body was also found in Youngstown by shipyard workers. Both of his legs were gone and his head was badly bruised and swollen.

Ice Bridge Tremble

Every winter, a huge, thick and usually reliable ice bridge forms across the Niagara River and reaches all the way from the United States to the Canadian side. On Sunday, February 4, 1912, there were about thirty people out on the bridge at about noon. "Tourists were encouraged to walk out on the ice bridge. Youngsters rode toboggans on the snowy mounds. Local business people set up shanties on the ice and sold souvenirs, lunches, tobacco and liquor. ... The ice bridge, 40-to-50-feet thick, was considered safe for pedestrian traffic and small shanties." (*The Niagara Falls Reporter*, Feb. 8, 2005 by Bob Kostoff)

Two of those people walking on the bridge were Eldridge Stanton and his wife Clara, both in their thirties, from Toronto, Ontario. They had been married for six years and came to visit Niagara Falls twice a year ever since, once in the winter and once in the summer. They walked hand in hand across the ice bridge. Also on the bridge were a couple of young boys from Cleveland, Ohio, Ignatius Roth and Burrell Hecock, both aged seventeen. William "Red" Hill opened the little refreshment stand he built every year. With him were Monroe Gilbert and William Lablond who were throwing snowballs and playing leapfrog.

A massive chunk of ice came sailing over the Falls and crashed down onto the ice bridge, causing the bridge's connection to come loose on both shores. Hill felt the tremor under his feet and knew that there was a serious problem with the bridge, so he called out to as many people as he could to run to safety. Lablond, Gilbert, and the two boys followed Hill towards the Canadian shore. Eldridge and Clara Stanton ran in the opposite direction towards the American shore. When Clara Stanton fell, her husband called out to the younger men to help him. Hecock went immediately to their aid, and Roth waited to see if that was enough help before he followed. The three people tried to move towards the American shore, but the ice that they were on was too far away from the land. They turned around and started to follow Roth, who needed a rope that Hill and Lablond threw out to him to pull him to safety through the icy water. Hecock and the Stantons were stranded on the ice bridge that started to head downstream.

The three people were seen talking to each other and pacing back and forth across the huge piece of ice, all the while Clara was holding her husband's hand. As they floated under the lower bridges, firemen, policemen and railway workers tried to lower ropes. They passed under three bridges and just as the ice seemed to get closer to the American shore again, they came across a hydro-electric station that was discharging water into the river. The pressure from this discharge crumbled the nearest edge of the ice forcing them to the opposite side, and the ice broke in half. It was the empty half that safely reached the shore. Just before the rapids, the ice broke in half again, separating Hecock from the Stantons.

Hecock's ice floated in the middle of the river, and railway workers lowered a rope for him. "He grabbed the rope and was dunked waist-high into the frigid water. Then the railroad men began slowly pulling him to the bridge some 190 feet above. Instead of just hanging on, Hecock attempted a hand-over-hand climb up the rope. People began to cheer as he moved closer and closer to safety, but the numbing cold took its toll and his hands began to slip. Hecock, in a last desperate attempt at life, tried to grasp the rope with his teeth. Then he fell, plummeting 30 feet to an ice floe. He stood up momentarily. A wave hit. He was washed over and disappeared into his icy grave, as spectators screamed and wept." (*The Niagara Falls Reporter*, Feb. 8, 2005 by Bob Kostoff)

The Stantons watched Hecock's attempts in horror. Eldridge was also able to grab a rope that was lowered down to them and tied it around Clara's waist. When the rope became taught, it snapped. He held his wife in his arms, kissed her, and they both knelt down together. They sped along on their piece of ice until they reached a huge wave in the rapids that overturned the ice they were on and threw them into the water one last time.

A Rigged Oar

On the morning of June 28, 1931, someone saw a rowboat headed towards the Canadian Rapids. He saw one man in the boat, and no oars. As the man in the boat tried to grab on to some ice as he floated by, the witness called the police. Two officers drove out to Goat Island and saw the boat immediately. They called for the firefighters to help, and the trucks drove up with ladders and ropes in hopes of making a rescue near Terrapin Rock. The boat was caught in the rapids and there was nothing anyone could so but watch as the man stood and frantically waved his arms right until the end.

That evening, William Hill Jr. found the wreckage. He also found an oar, but there was something strange about what he found. There was an old dirty trick where a person could saw part of an oar in half just enough that it would still work in weaker currents, but anything stronger would cause it to snap in half. There were also a lot of whiskey smugglers who crossed the waters around that time, and the competition was fierce. Police figured that it was probably caused by the competition or after some sort of betrayal, and it was meant to look like an accident. Nobody ever found out who did it, or who it was that died.

Cribwork Slip

I've often wondered when looking at the various bridges and structures around the Falls, how they were built under such dangerous conditions. Perhaps it was naive of me to think that everyone walked away from their jobs. In an attempt to divert water towards the Canadian Niagara Power Plant, the Northern Construction Company was working on removing cribwork from one of the submerged dams. On March 6, 1938, a thirty-three year old worker from Chippawa named Clarence Abt, stood on one of the fifteen ton cribs as it was lifted from the downstream side of the dam. He released the eight inch blocks he was carrying and started to clear the timber that was supposed to support the crib he was riding. The lumber accidentally moved and struck him across his body, sending him backwards into the water less than a thousand feet from the Falls.

Stunned for only a moment in the freezing water, Abt soon started swimming for his life. He was an expert swimmer, and started furiously fighting the current and headed towards the shore. Coworkers ran alongside the shore in hopes of throwing him ropes or buoys to rescue him. There was just not enough time and the current was too fast and strong, so Abt changed his plan and started to swim towards some of the rocks instead, hoping to give the others more time to save him. One of his coworkers said, "He fought to the last minute and made every possible effort to save himself. For a while it looked as if he might reach one of the rocks lying near the Falls and we could have rescued him. But the current carried him around, and the last I saw on him he had his right arm outstretched... it was awful." Mrs. Abt never liked where her husband was working and just knew something bad was bound to happen, she hoped he would never be taken away from her. He had been working on the dam since December, and died the day before his daughter's second birthday.

Power Out

There are theories that an earthquake in 1946 created a fissure or crack in the walls of the gorge. Jacob Schoellkopf had built a power plant in 1895, and built a second one right in front of it in 1956, without knowing about the fissure. Water leaked for ten years through the cracks in the walls, and it wasn't until June 7, 1956 that some workers noticed water getting into the plant itself. By that afternoon they had to round up forty men to haul sandbags to stop the flow of the water that was starting to widen the cracks and pour in.

It didn't take long for the Schoellkopf Power Station to lose two thirds of the plant in a disastrous collapse. By 5 p.m., the six generators that had produced 322,500 horsepower were destroyed and 400,000 kilowatts of power was lost from the grid. There was approximately one hundred million dollars damage overall. Richard Draper from Lewiston was killed. Right before the collapse, the men heard a loud rumble coming from behind the wall. The other workers were able to escape before the entire southern portion fell into the river. When the generators blew up, some of the debris flew so far it could be found on the Canadian side of the gorge. The remains of the Schoellkopf Station can still be seen from the Canadian side.

No Barrel

James Honeycutt, age forty, owned a house trailer about five miles upstream from the Falls at the Lynch Trailer Camp on the American side. He worked at the Niagara Parks Commission hydro project as a contractor, and enjoyed taking his fourteen-foot long aluminum boat out for rides along the river. He was friends with the Woodward family, and he would often take their two children, Roger (age 7), and his sister Deanne (age 17), along with him.

On July 9, 1960, the trio set out again for another boat ride. Everything was fine until the seven and a half horsepower outboard motor failed about a mile away from the Falls just as they were turning around to come back. The propeller pin had been sheared off. Immediately, Honeycutt told the children to put on their lifejackets, but he started rowing immediately back to shore and did not put one on himself. The boat capsized after hitting a shoal and a wave threw them over separating all three in the water. Deanne was pushed under again by a wave and when she resurfaced she could see two men on the shore. An auxiliary police officer and truck driver from New Jersey named John Hayes jumped over the rail. When Deanne heard John's voice screaming for her, she swam harder in his direction. Right before she went over the Falls, she was able to grab his thumb, but John knew that they would not be able to hold on that way for long and he shouted for more help. John Quattrochi, who also happened to be from New Jersey, climbed over the railing and pulled both of them in to the shore. They prayed for her brother. Deanne was taken to a the Memorial Hospital in Niagara Falls, New York, with a cut hand, and it wasn't until she got there when she learned about what happened to her little brother.

People could see Roger in the arms of Honeycutt as the water swept them towards the Horseshoe Falls. The two were separated as they went over the edge. Roger's running shoes came off of his feet about half way down, and he was only wearing a lifejacket and swimming trunks. He fell into the 180 foot deep water at the bottom of the Falls, but he quickly rose up to the surface again. Just before 1 p.m. the captain of the *Maid of the Mist II* (Clifford Keech) found Roger, and after three tries and in less than ten minutes they were able to pull him aboard with a life ring. He was taken to the Greater Niagara General Hospital in Ontario where he stayed for three days with a slight concussion.

Roger was the first to survive a trip over the Falls without a barrel.

James Honeycutt was not as lucky. He did not survive when he went over the Falls, and his body was found four days after the accident.

Thirty years later, Roger spoke to a church congregation about his ordeal and talked to them about what he remembered. "For me there was initially pure panic, I was scared to death. I can remember going through the Rapids and being thrown against the rocks and being bounced around like a toy in the water and being beaten up pretty badly. My panic very quickly shifted to anger and the anger was from seeing people running frantically up and down the shoreline and wondering why they wouldn't come out and rescue me." He said that after fear and anger, came peace. "There was a time I thought I was going to die and my seven years of life literally passed before me and I started thinking what my parents would do with my dog and my toys and had really given up at that point and felt I was going to die that afternoon." (http://www.infoniagara.com/other/history/roger.html)

Roger and Deanne told their story for a Canadian television special, and they also met up with her rescuers, both in their 80s, for a very emotional reunion.

In an effort to follow up on the story, "The Trivia Guys" from Ontario found out that, "The incident at the Horseshoe Falls was not Roger Woodward's only brush with death. In his junior year of high school in 1970, a tractor-trailer ran a red light and broadsided his motorcycle. He landed on a set of railroad tracks, escaping with only a broken finger on his left hand. In the fall of 1994, while on a night time boat trip across Lake Huron with his 9-year-old son, Jonathan, the pair became disoriented in a fog bank. Their boat was narrowly missed by a freighter." (*Whatever Happened To...? Catching Up With Canadian Icons* – http://www.triviaguys.com/)

Some people have very busy guardian angels.

The Pink Lady Failed

In 1961, Stanley and Gladys Tessman invited their friends, George and Jean Stewart, on a little cruise of the upper Niagara River on their sixteen-foot boat, *The Pink Lady*. They were headed upriver for the day, but on the way back their engine failed. As *The Pink Lady* entered the Canadian Rapids people could hear them calling out for help and screaming and as they dipped under the water and back up, all four passengers were clinging to the hull, right before the boat went over stern-first. A man and a woman were seen face-down in the rapids, and George Stewart was seen swimming for his life as hundreds watched and yelled out for him to make it. He was pulled under the Canadian Niagara Power Plant Bridge. Police raced to the scene with a rope to try to pull him out from underneath and just when they thought they had him, George lost his grip and disappeared. Hours later, most of his mangled body was removed from a turbine screen one hundred and forty feet underground. The next day, George Stewart's head and one of his arms were found below the Falls.

From Above

On February 11, 1963, four men were flying in a light airplane above Dufferin Islands, about three hundred yards from the Niagara River. They took off at about ten in the morning from St. Catherine's in a single engine Piper Tri-Pacer. There was a problem with the plane. There was a structural failure on the left wing that caused the plane to crash, and none of the four American men survived.

The Dry Discovery

The next story is about an accidental discovery of death. In the spring of 1969 the water was stopped over the American Falls by the U.S. Army Corps of Engineers. Geologists were excited to see what they could find out about the erosion of the Falls and whether or not it was worth removing any of the rocks below. Workers completed a dam between Goat Island and the mainland on June 11 and the water came to a stop. The next day, police found the body of a young male in the rocks—he had not been in the water for very long.

"There were no identifying marks or scars. The man wore a green shirt, black shoes, and black pants. The pants pockets had been turned inside out, probably due to the force of the falling water.

The American Falls.

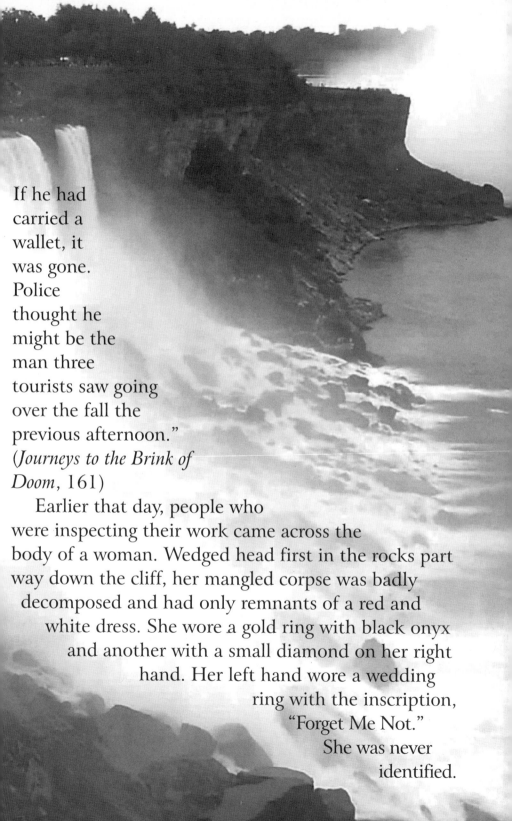

If he had carried a wallet, it was gone. Police thought he might be the man three tourists saw going over the fall the previous afternoon."
(*Journeys to the Brink of Doom*, 161)

Earlier that day, people who were inspecting their work came across the body of a woman. Wedged head first in the rocks part way down the cliff, her mangled corpse was badly decomposed and had only remnants of a red and white dress. She wore a gold ring with black onyx and another with a small diamond on her right hand. Her left hand wore a wedding ring with the inscription, "Forget Me Not." She was never identified.

182 Part Two: Death

Possible Gas Leak?

Edward Horning was operating an American sightseeing helicopter tour that ran from Goat Island. Horning was an experienced pilot with over 2,400 hours under his belt in the U.S. Navy. This is why I wonder if there was some sort of leak because the plane crashed when it ran out of fuel. An experienced pilot would not take off being so low on fuel that it only reached two hundred feet above the surface of the water. Witnesses say that they could see Horning struggling to regain control of the helicopter. His two passengers, Louis Episcopo and his companion Fillomena Pescatore, who were both in their fifties and from New Jersey, braced each other for a crash landing.

At 3:40 p.m. on August 5, 1969, the plane crashed into the upper Niagara River. None of the people on board survived. The two passengers floated free of the helicopter, but Horning's body was stuck inside the mangled machinery as it was swept through a hydro control dam before stopping on the Canadian shore one hundred yards downstream in calm water. Two more pilots came to the scene, Richard Carlin and Ernest Panapinto, and they were able to recover the bodies of Horning from the aircraft right away, and Pescatore was found by the Ontario Hydro staff. The body of Episcopo was found several days later at the bottom of the Horseshoe Falls.

White Water Rapid Running

On May 23, 1972, Niagara White Water Raft Company made their first successful run through the Whirlpool Rapids. Two days later, they invited people from the media, as well as friends and family to go along on a ride with them. Again, their trip was successful.

"In July of 1972, during a trial run, six passengers were thrown into the water of the Whirlpool Rapids. On August 5, 1972, during its maiden commercial voyage, a pontoon broke away from the raft and a passenger was plunged into the rapids. On August 13, 1972, seven people riding through the Whirlpool Rapids were thrown overboard. Luckily no fatalities were reported." (http://www.niagarafrontier.com/accident.html)

Despite their efforts to make the route safer and starting in Lewiston down to the Lower Rapids (by the Devil's Hole), the business shut down by September 1, 1972.

The Niagara Gorge River Trips Inc. was a white water rafting business that started some trial runs in 1975. They used a raft that was a prototype of a rubber raft made by the Zodiac Company of France. On the eleventh trial run on August 29, four staff including two pilots and twenty nine passengers went for a ride in the thirty-seven foot rubber and nylon raft. They left from the Maid of the Mist dock and were about two miles into their five-mile trip to Lewiston. When they reached the Whirlpool, the rubber raft capsized. All of the passengers were thrown free of the boat, and thirty of them survived with the help of emergency crews from both countries. Three people who got caught under the raft could not be saved: Julia Martinez, age thirty, of Toronto; David Ross, age thirty-seven, of Toronto, and Anthony Sawczyk, age twenty-four, of Niagara Falls, New York. A few of the survivors were taken to the Niagara Falls Memorial Medical Center with serious injuries.

Sadly, when the raft had to be recovered from the Whirlpool, the man who took the jet boat out had a heart attack and passed away.

When G and I went to see the Whirlpool, we could see the new Jet Boat Tours in the water. They did not go into the rapids that lead to the Whirlpool and stayed in the open and calmer areas in the water. Of course, the jet boats have been greatly updated since 1975 and they look much larger and safer. I even managed to get a short video while one was passing by in the water. It looked like a lot of fun, but we were strapped for time and weren't able to take a ride. If you're up for a thrilling ride, I do suggest you check out the Jet Boat Tours: http://www.whirlpooljet.com/

One of the Jet Boat Tours going past the Robert Moses Niagara Power Plant and Devil's Hole on the way to the calmer parts of the Whirlpool.

Unexpected & Brave Hero

I'd like to end this section of accidents with a story about a life that was saved by a hero who bears a name that we usually recognize as "Dr. Death." Back in 1912, a man named Henry Lutz, a candy maker from Buffalo, had a few too many drinks and decided to get some fresh air and go for a walk in Prospect Park. If he was sober, the slick ground from a recent rain would have been easy to avoid or manage, but unfortunately Henry slipped and fell into the water about one hundred and fifty feet from the edge of the American Falls. Also due to the recent rain, the water levels were high and he was immediately carried about fifteen feet from shore.

Luckily, there were two men who saw Henry's fall into the water: seventeen year old David Gordon, who was visiting the park with his father, and Iram Kevorkian, a 24-year old labourer. They both ran towards the slippery path while screaming for help. When they reached the bank at about one hundred feet downstream from Lutz, Gordon took one of the pike poles kept near the area for emergencies. When his father held him back from going into the water, Kevorkian took off his shoes and grabbed the pole from the younger man and went into the water. Gordon held Kevorkian's free hand at the edge of the water, and his father held his son's hand for dear life. As they were forming the human chain, Constable Thomas Harrington arrived and added his power to the chain as well.

Kevorkian stood in waist deep water as Lutz struggled in the current before falling face down in the water, head first towards the Falls. Despite Kevorkian's perfect

Just before the brink of the American Falls.

position ahead of him in the current, the water surged Lutz away from the edge once more. Kevorkian dove for him and risked his own life when his feet also slipped, but he was able to regain his balance quickly and still held on to the human chain tightly. Lutz became caught by a rock just long enough for Kevorkian to once again lunge towards him and snag him with the pole. The candy maker's pants ripped when he was pulled back, but the hook also penetrated his left leg. As he was being pulled back with the pole, more men showed up to add strength to the human chain and pulled Kevorkian's body towards the shore, which allowed him to get a two-hand grip on the pole, and Lutz was safely brought back to shore. Everyone was exhausted.

When police questioned Lutz down at the station, he told them his name was Henry Smith. He accepted the drink of whiskey offered to him to warm up, and promised that he would return to Buffalo immediately. However, as soon as he left headquarters we went back to drinking, and went back to Prospect Point. Not too long after that, John McGrath, a local produce worker, brought Lutz back to the police and reported a suicide attempt. Lutz was locked up and fell asleep as soon as he lay down on the bed. He was released by the courts to the custody of his son. Iram Kevorkian was awarded a medal by the Carnegie Hero Fund Commission.

Daredevils and Stunts

"Daredevil: 1. n. a person who is recklessly daring, esp. in order
to show off. 2. adj. daring in this way daredeviltry, daredevilry n.
ostentatious recklessness." (*Webster's Dictionary*, 244)

D aredevils, thrill seekers, and the need for ultimate
showmanship sometimes put the Darwinian
law of survival of the fittest into direct practice.
Although there are a number of people who have survived
incredible stunts above and over the Falls, there were
many casualties as well.

Despite all of the dangers there are still many people
willing to take the risk. Psychiatrist Lynn E. Ponton writes,
"American culture is defined at least in part by risk-taking
— westward expansion and the settling of the western
frontier were all about risk, and the successful pursuit of the
American Dream virtually requires taking risks. We are not a
culture that has ever been informed by the idea of carefully
assessing risks before taking them; after all, risk assessment
seeks to limit a certain kind of unbridled behaviour and so
runs counter to many of our myths about ourselves and our
history." (*The Romance of Risk*, 2)

Ponton focuses more on risk-taking teenagers and
preventative measures, but I believe a lot of what she
has to say can also be applied to the daredevils who
believe that pushing the boundaries is the only way to
achieve success in their lives. Erik Erikson also wrote
about adolescence and the need to create an identity,

but that they do not yet have the tools to master the transformation. After the War of 1812, and during a time when the countries of United States and Canada were so new and turbulent, Niagara Falls was stuck in the middle with no identity of its own. When a lot of the fighting had passed, there was a city filled with inhabitants who counted on their businesses to survive. The city needed an identity and one of the best options was to try to incorporate itself as a tourist destination. It was the birth of many daredevils willing to go over or do stunts around Niagara Falls.

Nowadays, if you're going to go over the Falls in a barrel, you might want to check up on some things first. In Hunter S. Fulghum's *Don't Try This At Home*, he dedicates one of the chapters to those who would like to know how to prepare themselves for a ride in a barrel. Here is a list of what you'll need:

- One barrel
- Protective clothing, including knee and elbow pads
- Helmet – a climber's helmet or football helmet with face guard will work well
- Mouth guard – chipped teeth are no fun and will ruin the post-success photos
- Cell phone or two-way radios with fresh batteries
- Important telephone numbers –
    weather information: 905-688-1847;
    Greater Niagara General Hospital: 905-358-0171
- One bottle of good champagne and Waterford crystal glasses
    – do not take champagne or glasses along in the barrel
- One flatbed truck with medium-duty crane
- Three to five friends
- Representatives of the media and/or someone who knows how to take good pictures
- Bail money

Of course, all of these supplies were not available back in the day when people first started to travel over the Falls in a barrel, and there are many styles of daredevilry and people who have tempted fate.

Francis Abbott

Francis Abbott came to be known as the Hermit of Niagara, a mysterious young Englishman who showed up on the American side of the Falls. He belonged to a respectable English family and his reason for leaving his old life was never known. Niagara Falls was already a popular tourist area when Abbott showed up in 1829. Many visitors found the Falls hypnotic, and perhaps that's what made Francis want to stay.

Tall, he walked with a gentleman's walking cane and with long strides. He wore a long cape that blew around behind him, but he was barefoot. He came to stay for a week at a small inn and brought only a few things with him; a bedroll, a book, a case for art supplies, and his flute. By the time he realized how overwhelming and irresistible the beauty and terrifying power of the Falls was, he wanted to stay longer, at least six months, but in total solitude.

Francis decided to stay on one of the Three Sisters Islands (just south of Goat Island at the top of the Falls), and made plans to build a small cabin. He wanted a drawbridge to make sure that anyone touring around Goat Island could not happen upon his private island. He was refused permission, but Augustus Porter owned Goat Island at the time and allowed Abbott to stay in an existing log cabin on the larger island. Excited, he packed his flute, a newly purchased violin, and some basic supplies.

For the most part, he kept to himself. Even when people called for him or tried to speak to him, he failed to answer. He wasn't being rude, he just fell silent for long periods of time. He played his flute or violin, and eventually he also bought a guitar to play all day long. His music would drift through the trees until the roar of the Falls drowned out the sound. He began to write his own songs, and people could hear him singing in Latin. He threw out anything he ever wrote right after he was done playing it. He eventually got a cat and a dog that he would take for walks around the island.

But there was nothing he was drawn to more than the Falls themselves. He did everything he could to get closer to the rapids. The nearby Terrapin rocks were connected to the island by a narrow bridge that ran right along the edge of the Falls. At the end of that narrow bridge, there was an eight inch squared piece of timber that stuck out beyond the rocks right on the edge, closer to the Canadian side of the river.

Very few tourists would dare to walk out on the narrow bridge out to the Terrapin Rocks, and if they did, none stayed for too long. They were too afraid that the bridge or railings would collapse and send them over the Falls.

Francis Abbott, on the other hand, walked out barefoot as he let his long hair blow around his face. Not only would he cross the bridge, but he would go out onto the lone wooden beam — sometimes pacing back and forth out there for hours. He was seen standing on the beam for hours on end, and sometimes balance on one foot or sit down and let his legs swing over the side. When he was in the mood, he would walk right to the very end and kneel down before holding on with only two hands while his body dangled over the Horseshoe Falls. People looked on in horror and screamed, but he could not hear them over the sound of the rushing water. He was just playing.

He had told someone in town once that what he was doing was the same thing a sailor would up in the high rigging of a ship during a storm. He wanted to rid himself of all fear.

Eventually he was not allowed to stay on Goat Island anymore, but instead of leaving Niagara he built a cabin on the American shore near a ferry dock (now Prospect Park). Every morning, even in the winter with chunks of ice floating by, he went for a swim/took a bath in the river. Two years after he'd arrived at his new location, Abbott went swimming three times on June 10, 1831—and the third time was his last. A ferry operator noticed that he had disappeared under the water after neatly folding his clothes on the shore, and he never came back up. Abbott was a strange man, and he didn't think too much of it until more time passed and he still didn't show above water. His body was swept downriver and over the edge into the whirlpool. For eleven days people watched, horrified as the body appeared in the mist only to be pulled back under again by the strong current. When the body was finally recovered, Francis Abbott was buried in Oakwood Cemetery in Niagara Falls, New York. The original headstone can't be read clearly anymore thanks to age and neglect. It once read:

Francis Abbott,
the Hermit of Niagara
Died June 10, 1831
He died in his 28th year

The area between Goat Island and the first Sister Island is now called the Hermit's Cascade, after Francis Abbott.

Avast, Ye Mates!

In the early 1800s, three vessels were sent over the Falls to create sublime spectacles to attract tourists. Schooners were large ships with sails and masts, and if you're familiar with the Canadian dime, the Bluenose on the back is a common example of a schooner.

By the 1820s there were three hotels catering to the visitors of Niagara Falls. William Forsyth of the Pavilion Hotel, with the help of John Brown of the Ontario House and General Parkhurst Whitney of the Eagle Hotel in Niagara Falls, New York, decided to pull the very first stunt in order to boost the tourism business. They acquired *The Michigan*, a condemned Lake Erie schooner sixteen feet from keel to the deck, that they prepared to send over the Falls in September of 1827. To make things more interesting, they put animals on board. Two bears, a buffalo, two raccoons, geese, two fox, cat, dog and other animals made a smaller version of Noah's Ark. They decorated *The Michigan* to look like a pirate's ship and even included a couple of human-shaped dummies tied to the deck.

Broadsheets were sent out to Western New York and Upper Canada that read:

> "The pirate Michigan with a cargo of ferocious wild animals will pass the great rapids and Falls of Niagara – 8th September 1827 at 6 o'clock."
>
> *The Michigan* has long braved the bellows of Erie, with success, as a merchant vessel: but having been condemned by her owners unfit to sail long proudly 'above'; her present proprietors, together with several public spirited friends, have appointed her to carry a cargo of Living Animals of the Forest, which surround the

upper lakes, through the white tossing and deep rolling rapids of Niagara and down its great precipice, into the basin 'below'. The greatest exertions are being made to procure animals of the most ferocious kind, such as Panthers, Wild Cats and Wolves; but in lieu of these, which it may be impossible to obtain, a few vicious or worthless dogs, such as may possess strength and activity, and perhaps a few of the toughest of the lesser animals will be added to, and compose the cargo...

"Should the vessel take her course through the deepest of the rapids, it is confidently believed that she will reach the Horse Shoe unbroken; if so she will perform her voyage to the water of the Gulf beneath which is of great depth and buoyancy, entire, but what her fate will be the trial will decide. Should the animals be young and hardy and possessed of great muscular power and joining their fate with that of the vessel, remain on board until she reaches the water below, there is a great possibility that many of them will have performed the terrible jaunt, unhurt!" (http://www.niagarafrontier.com/devil_frame.html#FIRSTSTUNT)

The ship was towed by Captain James Rough from Black Rock to Navy Island using the paddle steamer Chippawa. Here *The Michigan* was pointed towards the Falls in mid-river. Prior to the release of *The Michigan*, visitors were allowed to board the schooner and view the condemned animals. From about a quarter of a mile upstream the ship was cut loose. It held together over the first ledge, but over the second ledge the masts fell down and the ship started to break apart by the third ledge. It was turned around broadside and fell to thousands of pieces once it went over the Falls. One of the bears jumped from the ship and swam to the Canadian shore. One version of the story claims that the bear reached the water-logged ledge that broke into pieces and the bear fell down into the Falls after the ship. Another version claims that the bear was shot once it reached the Canadian banks, yet another story says there were two bears that managed to reach the island alive. Other than the bears, only two geese were said to have survived the trip as the rest of the animals were still caged or tied to the ship deck, or seen running up and down the deck before their demise. About fifteen thousand spectators were present for the spectacle.

In 1829 another schooner was sent over the Falls, but this time with no live passengers for the sake of amusement. The schooner *Superior* ended up getting caught at the top of the Falls lodged on the rocks at one of the islands for several days until the water re-floated the ship before it went over in pieces. The crowd was disappointed.

The third ship was called the *Detroit*, the flagship of Captain Barclay. It was captured in a naval victory on September 10, 1813 by Commodore Perry. The ship was brought down from Buffalo so that thousands could come to see the schooner go over, but they too, were disappointed. Near the last ledge, the *Detroit* also got caught in the rocks and started to dismantle. Part of the hull remained in place, stuck in the Falls. Over the years, pieces of the ship were torn off and disappeared. Unlike smaller ships that might be able to go over the ledges without falling apart, the large, old, and weak vessels never had a chance.

The *Caroline* was a different story. William Lyon Mackenzie (the first Mayor of Toronto until 1836) went to the Niagara Frontier after trying to organize a resistance against the Upper Canada government that was quickly overthrown. When he reached Buffalo, he began to organize his own government. Bonds were sold and the American supporters offered money and weapons, as well as the making of the steam vessel called the *Caroline* to transport supplies from the mainland to the Navy Island. Most of Mackenzie's three to four hundred American followers were unemployed.

Navy Island was Canadian Territory, and it is the only Canadian island in the Niagara River. When they heard about Mackenzie's strong presence on the island, the Upper Canada government sent Colonel Allan Napier MacNab and his militia to destroy their position. With the *Caroline* being the only way to transport to and communicate with the mainland, it was a prime target. MacNab sent a Royal Navy veteran, Lieutenant Andrew Drew, into American territory to Schlosser, New York where the ship was docked. "On 29 December 1837, during a night raid, the Canadian force invaded Schlosser (and, therefore, the United States), and set fire to the Caroline. One American, Amos Dufree, was killed during the attack. The blazing Caroline was set adrift and plunged to its complete destruction over Niagara Falls." (*The Niagara Frontier: Its place in U.S. and Canadian History*, 78)

With the War of 1812 not too far behind them, the American and Canadian sides nearly roused up the war once again because of the Navy Island attack. The British ended up paying the Americans for their losses. The Americans released Alexander McLeod, the militiaman who was on trial for murder. MacNab and Drew were knighted, and Mackenzie was arrested by the Americans for violating the Neutrality Act.

In Case You're Wondering

The first human to purposely go over the Falls as a stunt... survived. Sam Patch became the first human to challenge the Niagara River. On Wednesday October 7, 1829, Patch survived a dive into the rapids from a platform erected at a height of eighty-five feet. Patch tried the same feat again, this time from 130 feet on October 17th of the same year, and survived again.

Tightrope Trickery

Stephen Peer was born in Stamford Township in 1840. He was nineteen when he was inspired by Blondin's first performance of his many tight rope walking feats at Niagara Falls. Peer became determined to become the first real "Niagaran" to walk the Gorge. He became the assistant to the professional tightrope walker, Henry Bellini. When it came time to string the rope across the gorge, Peer was determined to be the first to tightrope walk across the Falls himself. Using Bellini's equipment (including a forty-eight pound, twenty-two foot long balance pole) without consent, Peer tried to walk the rope to spoil Bellini's attempt. Bellini tried to stop Peer by trying to cut the tight rope without success. Bellini was chased out of town, and everyone was rooting for the home town kid. Peer successfully crossed over and back to his starting point on the Canadian side on June 22, 1887 on a five-eighth inch diameter wire cable — the thinnest cable ever used across Niagara Gorge — and it was stretched between railway bridges, presently the Whirlpool Bridge and Penn Central Bridges. Three days later, Stephen Peer tried an unscheduled night time tightrope walk after an evening of drinking. More fantastical stories say that he was killed by rivals and thrown into the water, but his death remains a mystery. His body was found on the back of the river right below his wire cable.

A Sailor and a Challenge

Captain Matthew Webb was an experienced sailor who was also an excellent swimmer. Born in Shropshire, England in 1848, he was one of seven children. At the age of twelve years, Matthew Webb became a sea cadet on the naval training ship in Liverpool, England, and he had received medals for his bravery when shipmates were swept overboard.

Captain Webb also liked a challenge.

He swam the English Channel in 1875. When he came to Niagara Falls, he would be rewarded with $2,000 if he swam the Niagara River Whirlpool Rapids. On July 24, 1883, he was rowed out on the Maid of the Mist where he dove in and started swimming towards

The rapids leading to the Whirlpool.

This is where the rapids flow into the Whirlpool as seen from Whirlpool park.

the rapids and made it through with ease in about two minutes. Conflicting reports from eyewitnesses say that he didn't quite make it to the Whirlpool or that he was immediately sucked under by the Whirlpool where he died. Near Queenston, four days later, his mangled body was recovered. Captain Webb was buried at Oakwood Cemetery in Niagara Falls, New York.

Testing the Waters

Carlisle Graham survived the first trip in a barrel over the Falls on July 11, 1886. He made a second trip with his head outside of the barrel on August 19, 1886. The water in the rapids hit his head so hard that it damaged his eardrums and he partially lost his hearing, but he survived. On August 22, 1886, Carlisle Graham had offered ten dollars to James Scott to retrieve his barrel from the Whirlpool following his daredevil stunt. The day before the event, Scott decided to prepare for his task by making a practice jump into the water from a location west of Thompson's Point at the Whirlpool. Scott failed to resurface.

Tied to the Boat

Robert Flack came up with the idea that he could strap himself with harnesses to a small boat, which used his "secret" wooden shavings as a buoyant filling. He headed for the rapids on July 4, 1888. When his boat was overturned and he could not get himself free from the raft, he drowned.

The Dog Made It

Back to his old tricks, Carlisle Graham had another volunteer to work with him on a new stunt. Maud Willard got inside a barrel with her dog to travel through the Rapids and Whirlpool, while Graham swam behind the barrel the entire way. When the barrel reached the middle of the whirlpool it got stuck in the swirl of the water for six hours. The barrel reached the shore intact. When they opened it up, Maud's dog jumped out unharmed. Maud Willard had suffocated because her dog put its nose to the only air hole, and there was no air entering the barrel for her at all.

> "The same CPR technique used for humans can be adapted to save the life of a dog. CPR will provide heart contractions and breathing until the dog can perform these functions on its own... Hold the dog's mouth and lips closed. Apply a muzzle. Inhale and put your mouth over the dog's nose, forming an airtight seal. Exhale. Repeat the process 10-15 times per minute. Remove your mouth and apply heart massage in between breaths. Place the heel of one hand over the dog's chest (in line with the back of its elbow). Place the heel of your other hand on top of the other. Pump firmly and briskly. Hold each push for two counts and release for a count of one. (Use pressure appropriate for the size of the dog.)" (dog.com)

I wonder if Carlisle Graham was not the best person to work with when it came to stunts including Niagara Falls. It also makes me wonder why Maud didn't pull the dog away from the air hole for six hours.

Demon Barber of Bristol
& the Anvil

I can't possibly leave out a story about someone with the nickname "Demon Barber of Bristol." Known in England for his high dives and parachute jumps from a balloon and kissing a lion, he still wasn't receiving the fame and money wanted and needed to support his family, let alone to live the high life.

Charles Stephens came to Niagara Falls with his wife, Annie, and eleven children. He'd decided at the age of fifty-three that he was going to go over the Falls in a barrel. He had personally supervised as the six foot, three inches tall and quarter of a ton barrel was constructed in London. The heavily padded interior had electrical lighting and his friends tried to talk him into taking an eight hour oxygen supply. He was a stubborn man, but finally agreed. Stephens also knew that he needed a ballast, something heavy to enhance the stability of the barrel. He decided on a hundred pound anvil that he tied to his feet as his friends looked on in amazement and horror. When others suggested that he send the barrel over empty first as a test, he thought they were trying to thwart his attempts and inevitable success.

On July 11, 1920, Stephens put on his padded suit, an air cushioned vest and a thick wool hat. He tied himself to the anvil and gathered six pillows around him for extra protection in the barrel. He knew the police would try to stop him, so without a raucous fanfare he started his journey at eight in the morning in front of a small audience. A Toronto motion picture company was invited to film his stunt, and boarded a motorboat to follow with his assistants. One hundred yards from shore, one of the iron hoops broke off, but the crew determined that the barrel was still safe enough to finish the trip. About an hour later, Charles went over the Falls. What he didn't expect, was to have the barrel tip upside down on its way over, sending him head first with the anvil still tied to his foot.

"Tourists, camera men, police authorities, tour guides, and experienced rivermen all watched and waited for Stephens to emerge from the billowing white cloud at the foot of the Horseshoe..." When the barrel reached the bottom of the waterfall, the anvil was thrust through the top of the barrel, taking most of Stephens with it. When the barrel finally broke apart and the rest of the iron rings came loose, the pieces were recovered. "...An examination of the wood of which Stephens's barrel had been constructed revealed it to be dry and brittle. Riverman William 'Red' Hill Sr. expressed the opinion that the barrel had been held at the bottom of the Horseshoe by the falling water until the staves failed. He opined that Stephens's body would surface only when the straps holding his feet to the anvil broke or disintegrated." (*Journeys to the Brink of Doom*, 62)

On July 12, a United States Immigration Inspector pulled out a man's right arm at the Maid of the Mist dock. It had been torn from the shoulder of Demon Barber of Bristol. The tattoo on his forearm read: Forget Me Not Annie. His arm is buried in an unmarked grave in the Drummond Hill Cemetery.

At the age of eighty-one, his only surviving child waited until 1991 to return to Niagara Falls, where she had watched him die.

The Mystic and the Turtle

George Strathakis was a forty-six year old bachelor originally from Greece, where he became a religious mystic. He claimed to have stood at the North Pole and said, "I am king and master of the earth, and from this summit I am going to rule and direct it." He also said he had been born in central Africa on the banks of River Abraham in the tenth century. He also had a pet turtle named Sonny that he claimed was 150 years old and was supposed to have been sacred to a mysterious Greek cult.

Living in Buffalo, New York, George worked as a chef, but he wanted to become a full time writer and sell his books on metaphysical experiences. His book, *The Mysterious Veil of Humanity Through the Ages*, was about his unbelievable history, and it was written in a totally incoherent way as if it was the work of a madman. He needed to find a way to raise some money so that he could publish and sell his books. (Those crazy writers.) Strathakis would often take a rowboat closer and closer to the edge, inspired by the success and even the failures of people like Stephens who had ridden a barrel over the Falls. He copied Stephens' design using wood and iron rings and made a very large vessel that was ten feet long and five feet in diameter. It was a heavily padded steel cylinder with four inch thick staves held together by steel hoops with a hatch at one end. He strapped himself to a spring mattress, brought an oxygen tank that would last eight hours, and included his best friend, 150 year old turtle, Sonny. Red Hill had told him that there was too much surface area, and that the weight of the barrel at nearly a ton, would not endure the trip over the Horseshoe Falls.

On July 5, 1930 at 3:30 p.m., George left from Navy Island and rode over the Falls expecting the whole trip to take two hours. He was so sure he was going to succeed and stay on schedule that he'd made reservations and ordered a steak dinner at the Manhattan Restaurant in Niagara Falls, New York. Red Hill and his son waited at the Maid of the Mist landing for Strathakis to emerge. Hours went by and the *Maid of the Mist* made two trips to the bottom of the Horseshoe Falls to look for him. At four in the morning, the Hills went home to get some sleep. At 1:30 p.m. on July 6, Red Hill recovered the body. The barrel was undamaged; however, it just got caught behind the wall of water for over twenty-two hours (it took an additional six hours to get the barrel hatch open). George had suffocated. Sonny, the turtle, survived.

"Turtles aren't as complicated to care for, but many die in captivity because they aren't treated with the same degree of care and attention their fur-bearing counterparts. If they are properly cared for, turtles can live for many decades, but this requires you pay close attention to their diets, living arrangements, and treatment. Making sure a turtle has enough room to live in, making sure it has enough light, shade, and moisture, clean water, and a basking lamp are just a few of the steps you need to undertake to keep your pet turtles healthy... As far as water is concerned, avoid using tap water for your turtle tank, as chlorine and fluoride are present in tap water, and can disturb the ph balance. Use natural spring water for your turtle's drinking water, and de-chlorinated water for the swimming area." (petturtle.com)

I don't think it matters if George ever read any turtle care instructions. He should have taken more time planning out all possibilities and increased his own chances of survival. Perhaps people should consider not taking their pets over the Falls? It seems to be bad luck.

Hills and Barrels

In order to tell you the story about William "Red" Hill Jr., I have to let you know a little bit more about his father, William "Red" Hill Sr. At forty-two years old, Hill Sr. fulfilled his promise and took on the Rapids and Whirlpool. Having been born and raised in Niagara Falls, the Gorge was a playground to him. This made him much more knowledgeable about the waters than anyone else. He used a six foot long steel barrel to make his second successful journey from the Maid of the Mist landing to Queenston (his first was in 1910) with only the slight snag of becoming caught in the vortex of the Whirlpool and had to be pulled free by his son and friends before finishing his journey. Using a similar barrel with harnesses, Hill Sr. made a third trip on Memorial Day in 1931. Not only did the barrel start to leak and fill up half way, it got stuck in the vortex of the Whirlpool again. Using a rope tied around his waist to tie onto the barrel, Hill Jr. swam out to the barrel and once again, saved his father.

When he wasn't tempting the waters himself, Hill Sr. received more Lifesaving Awards than anyone else in history from the Canadian Government. He saved twenty-eight people from drowning. Hill Sr. also recovered one hundred and seventy-seven accident or suicide victims, and he could swim from the foot of the American Falls to the Canadian shore in eleven minutes. There are many stories of his heroism, and right alongside was his son, Red Hill Jr. who had some very large shoes to fill. He had helped his father during most of the twenty-eight rescues and the recovery of the bodies of all of the suicide and accident victims. On his own he recovered an additional twenty-eight bodies from the waters, and he even tried to beat his father's eleven minute swimming record from the American Falls to the Canadian shore, and failed. There was one more thing he needed to do to follow his father's legacy—he had to get in a barrel himself.

His first successful attempt took place on July 8, 1945 in front of two hundred thousand people. For his second attempt, he had to create a diversion so that the police could not stop the stunt. Hill Jr. announced that he would be departing from the docks of the Maid of the Mist at two in the afternoon, when in fact he had been lowered upstream into the Gorge shortly after two. The barrel got caught in forty-two mile per hour currents and, before it even reached the Rapids, a cross-wave hit the barrel sending it flying up into the air where it somersaulted twice before coming back down. He got stuck in the vortex of the Whirlpool and his brothers had to row out and pull him to shore before he finished his trek to Queenston. Two and a half hours later, he arrived safely. That night he went to put flowers on his father's grave, and later in the evening his mother suffered a (non-fatal) heart attack.

On September 6, 1948, Hill Jr. tried again using a barrel that weighed close to a thousand pounds. Once again a cross-wave hit the barrel, this time sending it forty feet into the air. His brother once again had to pull the barrel out of the vortex after it had been completely pulled under a few times. Badly bruised, Hill Jr. bailed out water for an hour before continuing his stunt. Fame came for him, but money did not, and all of the barrels and materials were confiscated and sold. He had to continue the legend and try to regain some financial status. The next time, he tried a steel torpedo-shaped barrel.

Hill Jr. challenged the Rapids again in July of 1949 at the age of thirty-eight. The steel took a massive pounding and Hill Jr. had to be lifted in a basket from the Gorge and taken to hospital. It was a failure both in terms of fame and fortune. The unfulfilled desire to follow in his father's path and restore the legend drove Red Hill Jr., and he felt that he only had one last option. He had to go over the Falls—something his father would never attempt.

He had no money, and could not build a proper barrel. Instead, he constructed what he called "The Thing" in the summer of 1951, consisting of thirteen large, heavy duty inner tubes held together with three inch wide canvas webbing, which was then covered in heavy fish netting. He painted it silver and wrote "The Thing" all around the tubes. He told the *Buffalo Courier-Express*, "The truck inner tubes should cushion the shock. If the wind's right and I can get the breaks, I'll come out okay. (Lifts a beer bottle) Here's for luck!" Three miles upstream of the Horseshoe Falls he launched from Ushers Creek on the Canadian side. When he went over the brink, the massive crowd went silent. The weight of the water falling on the tubes broke them apart and two minutes after hitting the bottom, they resurfaced. The silence of the crowd was shattered when his mother screamed out for him from above. His wife and ten year old daughter then joined her, and his brothers began the dreadful task of searching for his body. *The Thing* was shredded and his brother found only his shoes in the netting. Hill's brothers, Major Norman and Wesley, searched for him. It wasn't until the next morning that his beaten body was found by the Maid of the Mist dock.

Boys and Adventures

On May 11, 1970, three eleven year old boys, Gary, David, and Richard, set out for an adventure. They walked several blocks from their homes and climbed two chain link fences, bringing them about a mile from the American Falls. They found a large, wooden industrial shipping skid. It was big enough to work as a raft for all three boys, but first, they had to get it into the water. They flipped the twenty-by-eight platform end over end. After all their hard work, all three boys climbed aboard and pushed away from shore. They were barely one hundred feet out when they realized that the seemingly calm water had a quicker current than they realized. They immediately decided to head back for shore, but only two of them could swim. David remained on the raft, figuring his chances were better since he would surely drown if he tried to swim. The other two made it back to shore and flagged down a car, and the driver called the police.

When officers Anthony Laratta and Arthur Woodhead arrived, they immediately tried to get in the water to reach the raft but it was too far out. They raced back to their cars hoping to intercept the raft from the American Rapids Bridge that connected Goat Island with the mainland. Officers Donald Stewart and Richard Sutliffe also arrived on the bridge just in time to see the raft coming towards them in the white water. The path never strayed towards either shore. The raft went under the water, and when it came back up the boy was not on it anymore. People ran along the shore yelling for David to hold on, to hang on. It was too late. David went over

the American Falls before anyone could save him. When witnesses were interviewed afterwards, most commented on how helpless they felt, how everything happened so quickly, and how they didn't realize the true force of the river.

The water rushing towards the American Falls where they tried to catch David.

Mr. X

"It's a very dangerous thing to believe in nonsense."
— *James Randi*

He survived, but I have to include this story. The man that so many people my age have only known as a Paranormal Investigator and Ghost Debunker was also a stuntman as well as a magician. Since 1946, James Randi worked as a magician and escapologist under his original name, Randall Zwinge. (During Alice Cooper's 1974 tour, Randi performed as the dentist and executioner on stage. Randi had also built and designed several of the stage props, including the guillotine.) Specifically, I had personally never heard that James Randi once suspended himself over Niagara Falls in a straightjacket. (I was just over a year old at the time.) On February 7, 1975, Randi hung from a crane at the Table Rock over the Horseshoe Falls for five minutes in the freezing cold. He was working for a Toronto film company at the time, and it was performed for a Canadian television program called "World of Wizards." They had permission from the Niagara Parks Commission to conduct the stunt. Obviously, he escaped the straightjacket.

Slowing the Rapidman

Jessie W. Sharp was seventeen when he first thought about riding over the Falls in a kayak in 1979. He went so far as to talk to a reporter and photographer from *United Press International*. His wise and probably very upset family brought him back to Tennessee immediately. By the time he was twenty-eight, Jessie was an expert kayaker who had already tackled forty-foot cataracts and Class 4 rapids (the worst are similar to those at Niagara, which are Class 6). Obsessed with the Falls, unemployed, and wanting to further his career as a stunt man, he brought his twelve foot long, thirty-six pound polyethylene kayak named "Rapidman" to Niagara Falls after planning his stunt for three years. The goal was to gain enough speed to be thrown out over the Falls and land in the pool below, clearing the crashing waters altogether. He brought a film crew with him and hoped to catch not only the trip over the Falls, but also through the Rapids and Whirlpool afterwards. He was so confident in his success and timing that he had made dinner reservations at the Queenston Park Restaurant after docking in Lewiston. Just to make sure his face wasn't covered, Jessie did not wear a helmet. He also didn't wear a lifejacket so that he would be able to squirm out easily if he got caught under the Falls. He was filmed going over the Niagara Falls on June 5, 1990.

"Powerhouse operators diverted the water from the river in an effort to ground the Rapidman, but Sharp was undeterred. He simply maneuvred around the rocks

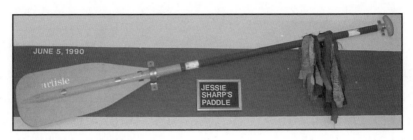

Jessie Sharp's Paddle.

exposed by the low water level, and headed toward the center of the fall. The attempt to stop him had only one effect, and that was to slow him down. Just as Sharp reached the brink he raised his paddle above his head and twirled it in one hand, then, at 1:45 pm, he plunged into the mist and vanished." (*Journeys to the Brink of Doom*, 72)

By three that afternoon, the kayak popped up just under the Falls. His body has never been discovered.

Jet Ski, Rocket, Parachute

Robert Overacker came from California with his jet ski and a rocket. Robert was a graduate of a California stunt school who raced cars at Ventura Raceway. Friends knew that he had been planning the stunt for seven years. One of the reasons why he did the stunt was because he wanted to draw attention to the homelessness in the world and raise awareness. His jet ski was decorated with stickers that read SAVE THE HOMELESS. On October 1, 1995, at thirty-nine years old, Overacker followed out his stunt as planned. He rode his jet ski to the brink of the Falls and just before he went over, he deployed a rocket that he had strapped to himself to open up his parachute that would allow him to float to the waters below before

Robert Overacker's Jet Ski where "Save the Homeless" is clearly labelled, and it also says above and in a smaller text "Firecracker Overacker."

being rescued. I've personally gone parachuting before (I told you before I'm a bit of a "Type T" myself), and when we were being trained I remember the instructors saying that you should always pack your own parachute to make sure it's done properly. (They supervised us as we did it.) It seems that Robert Overacker did not take this extra precaution. The rocket did employ and successfully fired out with the parachute following behind it. What he didn't realize was that the parachute was not attached or tethered to his body as it flew away behind him. Other reports say that the rocket failed to discharge at all as he fell 180 feet to the water (which is like hitting cement, said police at the time). His step-brother and friend were in attendance during his stunt. His body was recovered by the staff aboard the *Maid of the Mist*. "Overacker, married with no children, became the fifteenth person since 1901 to intentionally go over the Falls in or on a device." (http://www.infoniagara.com/other/daredevils/robert.html)

Doing Your Own Stunts...

If you'd still like to try this stunt of going over the Falls after everything you've read, I'll tell you some more about what Hunter S. Fulghum suggests for this little trip. You have to build your own barrel because you're not going to be able to purchase one that's fit for the drop.

He suggests, "Build it of 3/16 inch reinforced steel, watertight with an access hatch... the weight of the hatch must not exceed 40 pounds, which is the maximum most people can lift with one arm. The barrel should be approximately four-five feet in diameter, eight-twelve feet long, with rounded ends to help prevent the barrel from hanging up on the rocks... Ballast (no more than 300 pounds) and keel (3 inches) are recommended... Air supply suitable for 90-120 minutes. This can be supplied by one or two scuba tanks... Provide two-inch nylon webbing straps to secure yourself during the trip." (*Don't Try This At Home*, 70)

The amount of detail that he includes beyond what I have quoted is very well researched and specific to the job. The next step is the actual launch using the truck into the area by the Whirlpool Bridge. After that, hold on tight and don't arch your back to protect against impact, "Stay calm and loose." Of course! Being stressed out and clinging for dear life should help you stay calm. The drop over the Falls takes about three seconds, and in theory, you should come back up to the surface very quickly. Wait a few minutes or more before opening the hatch or else you could flood the barrel and sink.

CELEBRATE YOUR CONTINUED LIFE

"Step out of the barrel. Take the bottle of chilled champagne from one of your assistants and shake it vigorously. Spray everyone within 15 feet in celebration of being alive. (Then,) Surrender to the authorities." (*Don't Try This At Home*, 72)

"In some cases the effect of the falling waters is so great as to inspire an almost uncontrollable desire to leap into the foaming tide. It is perhaps this power of the cataract to lure to self-destruction that the Indians tried to explain in their legend that the Falls demand four victims annually."
— *Charles Mason Dow, 1917*

Conclusion...*Until Next Time*

People come from all over the world because they are drawn to Niagara Falls. You might visit on your honeymoon, on your way across the border to other destinations, or simply to see this incredible wonder of the world. G and I used to go on dates and have picnics in the parks when we were younger, and we still enjoy visiting as much as we can.

Mark Twain found great inspiration, James Randi found a great audience, and many other people have become famous because of the Falls. I have only included the stories about the people who did not survive but there are many successful heroes and stunt stories for you to see, and you can marvel at their techniques and motives. There are museums for you to learn all about the history of the area, and you can spend some time (and money) at the casinos if that's your game. Go and check out the Whirlpool, and if you are physically able, climb down some stairs in the Devil's Hole. Don't forget to take a ride on the *Maid of the Mist*, and if you're up for it, whip out on a Jet Boat Tour or go into the Cave of Winds for more of a thrill. There are also many tourist attractions and some great restaurants on Clifton Hill. Enter into the "haunted" houses if you dare! Or, you could spend some time with some real ghosts.

Niagara-on-the-Lake is also a beautiful and quaint place to spend some time. Offering everything from antique shops and the Shaw Festival, more wonderful restaurants and historical sites to see, it's definitely worth spending a few days. Now that you know where some of the haunted places are, you can seek them out, or try to avoid them. Check out some of the walking tours such as the ones run by Haunted Hamilton, or Kyle Upton's Walking Ghost Tour of Fort George. Wave to the Lady in White down at the beach by the Gazebo, and give Captain Swayze a message for me: tell him that I'll be back.

I've shared with you some of the stories in and around the Niagara area, and although there are many more to be found I hope you enjoyed this collection. You might have changed your mind about ghosts, and you might have a new perspective on the power of the Falls. I hope you get a chance to go and discover your own experiences and feelings while surrounded by the spirits and death in Niagara.

Bibliography

Bernat, Clark and Joy Ormsby. *Niagara-On-The-Lake*. St. Catherine's, Ontario: Looking Back Press (an imprint of Vanwell Publishing Limited), 2003.

Berton, Pierre. *Niagara: A History of the Falls*. Toronto, Ontario: McClelland & Stewart Inc., 1992.

Blauner, Susan Rose. *How I Stayed Alive When My Brain Was Trying To Kill Me: One Person's Guide to Suicide Prevention*. New York, New York: Quill (an imprint of HarperCollins publishers), 2002.

Columbo, John Robert. *Ghost Stories of Ontario*. Toronto, Ontario: Hunslow Press, 1996, 2nd Printing.

More True Canadian Ghost Stories. Toronto, Ontario: Prospero Books, 2005.

Mysterious Canada. New York, New York: Doubleday, 1988.

Davies, Charles W. *Romance of Niagara*. Stevensville, Ontario: M&D Publishing, 2000.

Fulghun, Hunter S. *Don't Try This At Home: How to win a Sumo Match, Catch a Great White Shark, Start an Independent Nation, and Other Extraordinary Feats (for Ordinary People)*. New York, New York: Broadway Books, 2002.

Greenhill, Ralph and Thomas D. Mahoney. *Niagara*. Toronto, Ontario: University of Toronto Press, 1969.

Higgins, Robert. *The Niagara Frontier: Its Place in U.S. and Canadian History*. Kitchener, Ontario: Upney Editions, 1996.

Hines, Terence. *Pseudoscience and the Paranormal: A Critical Examination of the Evidence*. New York, New York: Prometheus Books, 1988.

Holzer, Hans. *Ghosts: True Encounters with the World Beyond, Haunted Places, Haunted Houses, Haunted People*. New York, New York: Black Dog & Leventhal Publishers, 1997.

Jackson, John N. with John Burtniak and Gregory P. Stein. *The Mighty Niagara, One River – Two Frontiers*. Amherst, New York: Prometheus Books, 2003.

Kearney, Mark, and Randy Ray. *Whatever Happened To...? Catching Up With Canadian Icons*. Toronto, Ontario: Hounslow Press, 2006.

Kriner, T. W. *Journeys to the Brink of Doom: The Stories of True Disaster, Mystery, and Heroism at Niagara Falls*. Buffalo, New York: J&J Publishing, 1997.

Mady, Najla. *BOO! Ghosts I Have(n't) Loved*. Toronto, Ontario: New Canada Publications (a division of NC Press), 1993.

Molto, Kimberly. *True Tales of the Paranormal: Hauntings, Poltergeists, Near-Death Experiences, and Other Mysterious Events*. Toronto, Ontario: Dundurn Press, 2002.

Nelson, Richard E., PhD. and Judith C. Galas. *The Power to Prevent Suicide: A Guide for Teens Helping Teens*. Minneapolis, Minnesota: Free Spirit Publishing, 1994.

Ponton, Lynn E., MD. *The Romance of Risk: Why Teenagers do the Things they Do*. New York, New York: BasicBooks, a division of HarperCollins Publishers Inc., 1997.

Randi, James. *James Randi: Psychic Investigator*. London, England: Boxtree Limited, 1991.

Rule, Leslie. *Coast to Coast Ghosts: True Stories of Hauntings Across America*. Kansas City, Kansas: Andrews McMeel Publishing, 2001.

Smith, Barbara. *Ontario Ghost Stories*. Toronto, Ontario: Lone Pine Publishing, 1998.

Sulloway, Frank J. *Freud Biologist of the Mind: Beyond the Psychoanalytic Legend*. New York, New York: Basic Books Inc. Publishers, 1979.

The New Lexicon Webster's Encyclopedic Dictionary of the English Language, Canadian Edition. New York, New York: Lexington Publications, Inc., 1988.

Upton, Kyle. *Niagara's Ghosts 2*. St. Catherine's, Ontario: Self Published, 2004.

Walsh, Darryll. *Ghost Waters*. East Lawrencetown, Nova Scotia: Pottersfield Press, 2002.

Wolman, Benjamin B. (Editor) with Laura. A. Dale, Gertrude R. Schmeidler, Montague Ullman. *Handbook of Parapsychology*. Jefferson, North Carolina: McFarland & Company, Inc., Publishers, 1977

Woog, Adam. *Poltergeists: Great Mysteries, Opposing Viewpoints*. San Diego, California: Greenhaven Press, Inc., 1995